THE *Blessed* House

By Barbara Malone

PublishAmerica
Baltimore

First printing

PublishAmerica has allowed this work to remain exactly as the author intended, verbatim, without editorial input.

ISBN: 978-1-61546-692-4 (softcover)
ISBN: 978-1-4489-6662-2 (hardcover)
PUBLISHED BY PUBLISHAMERICA, LLLP
www.publishamerica.com
Baltimore

Printed in the United States of America

For my family who lived in
and
my friends who dined in

The Blessed House

Acknowledgments

I wish to thank Mari Messer, a talented generous author, who gave me inspiration, guidance, encouragement and valuable criticism. I thank the members of the Vanderbilt Beach Library Writers Workshop of Naples, Florida for their perceptive comments and support. I also thank my good friend, Jackie Markham, who generously and expertly typed this manuscript and to her husband, Bob, who did the graphics and pictures. Thanks to Carol Albright for her support and expertise.

Cheers to my 'test pilots' who listened to me read pages of material as I wrote; my family, my friends and the Ladies On The Beach. They filled me with laughter and constancy.

Come, you who are blessed by my Father. Inherit the kingdom prepared for you from the foundation of the world.

Matthew 25

Prologue

This Blessed House is about a house where God bestows special healing and nurturing blessings to the family who lives in it, the friends who visit it and the clients who come seeking peace. I live in this landmark with the million-dollar view of the Greenwich Bay waters. I continue to feel the spirits of the Priest who lived and said Mass in it and the parishioners who worshiped God in it and built it sixty-eight years ago.

There is humor and pathos in these stories about our family rebuilding the house together; our friends quahogging, wind surfing and sailing in our front yard and eating spaghetti and meatballs; and those who come for counseling in my office in the Blessed House.

Inspiration and hope are plentiful and flourish in these stories about how the Holy Spirit continues to dwell in our house, healing family from past childhood pain, job loss, divorce, death and emotional crisis long after the Priest died.

Love blazoned throughout the book; our love for God, our love for each other as spouses, our love for our family and our love for our neighbor.

Some names have been changed to protect the privacy of some individuals.

Table of Contents

Book I

History of Our House
and Renovations

For I was hungry and you gave me food.

CHAPTER 1
The Altar Boy's Story

Father St. Jean dropped dead of a heart attack in the former kitchen, now a library-office, of the house he built, our Blessed House.

When we bought this house our knowledge of its history was limited to knowing that a priest owned this summer house and said Mass on Sundays on an altar on a raised platform in an alcove of the living room. When he died, the neighbor, Frank, bought the house, installed central heating and rented it to a carnival family for a few years.

One day, after we had been living in this house for twenty years, an older gentleman was walking around our property gazing at the house. My husband engaged him in conversation.

"I was an altar boy many years ago and I helped to build this house. I was curious to see if it was still here," he said. We invited him to look around at the extensive changes we made and in return he revealed the unknown history of our home, like where the priest died. He continued,

"In 1939 they were wrecking our wooden church, St. John's in West Warwick. They were building a larger modern church. Many of the parishioners, altar boys and I carted the old, knocked-down lumber from the demolition site in trucks and cars to this spot in Buttonwoods. The parishioners and the priest built this house. I was about ten years old."

Tom and I were amazed and captivated by his story. We listened intently to him. "When we were building this house, the women fished, clammed and cooked for the workers. At the end of the day we gathered together to eat on the grassy slope above the water right there," he pointed underneath the huge maple tree.

"Where did they get the beautiful knotty pine for the walls throughout the house?" my husband inquired.

"The priest owned a small cabin in the campground a few yards away. The people dismantled the walls in the cabin for some of it, probably had to buy more for this size house," he answered."The outer walls were all from the Church."

"Did you go to Mass here?" I asked.

"Yes, after the house was built the priest would say Mass in the morning in the living room. Then everyone went clamming or fishing. Bluefish and soft-shell clams were plentiful as well as littlenecks and quahogs. Of course, the women did all the cooking. Later in the day we would all eat at a long table in the Banquet Room. What a feast we had every weekend: clamcakes, chowder, stuffies, pasta. As a kid, it was great fun because we went swimming and running around on the beach. It was like a vacation," he reminisced.

We continued our tour to the lower level. The refurbished recreation room now has a ping pong table, couches, computer and desk. We walked into the former second kitchen which is now a laundry room and full bathroom. I was curious and asked, "What was the kitchen on this level for?"

"They needed two kitchens to do the cooking for all the guests," he explained. "They came to swim and cool off in the summer, a respite from the heat."

We climbed the stairs to the second floor. We showed him the two bedrooms that we added. He marveled when he saw our bedroom-sitting room with our king size bed, couch, desk and adjoining bathroom.

"You know this was a closed-in porch. The view is still spectacular. I think this room was for quiet talking and praying."

I can see why they would enjoy this oasis, former sun porch, for serene contemplation and the view of the beach and waters below. This is my special place: my place to meditate, to pray, to write and sleep. Now I know why I feel the spirits of the people before me in this room: surrounding me, inspiring me and bringing me peace and love.

When the Altar Boy was leaving the house he said,

"Thank you for the tour. You know it still feels like the Priest's house." I sighed thinking that was the best compliment he could have given us.

If we were having any doubts about the Altar Boy's story, coincidently, two months later another elderly gentleman unexpectedly arrived and corroborated his story.

When our parish priest blessed our house soon after we moved in, we were unaware that we were living in such a Blessed House. The Altar Boy's revelations lead me to understand why I feel so good when I go clamming, cooking and feeding people on these very grounds, just like the original settlers. A tradition was started long before the house was built and we have been joyfully, unknowingly, continuing this rite for the past twenty years. I feel the history wrapped around me. We fit like a hand in a glove. Can we continue these traditions in the Blessed House?

Three years ago I met an elderly neighbor. She and I were walking on the beach in front of my house discussing the erosion and land loss of my property due to winter storms.

"I remember when there was no house on the hill here. I was a teenager then. There were bathhouses on your beach," she confided to me. "We used them to change our bathing suits when we went swimming. There were cement steps in front of the bathhouses leading to the water. This was our teenage hangout. That was about seventy-five years ago. The great New England hurricane of 1938 washed them away. What a fun place it was!" she exclaimed.

I still think it is a fun place to live. I am so fascinated by the stories about my house. There are more discoveries to come.

"When are you going to build a wall to stop the erosion?" my neighbor, who lives three houses behind me, asked. "Pretty soon I'll have waterfront property," she continued sarcastically.

For twenty years we enjoyed our white sandy beach: swimming, sunbathing, digging clams, burying clambakes and mooring boats. We could walk out our front door down the sloping hill to the beach. The winter storms raged as well as one hurricane; taking with them fifty feet of our land.

The rolling green hill of grass is now a sharp cliff. The wooden walkway, built by our sons, lies smashed and in pieces leaning against the remaining hill. One bunch of violet wild flowers survive; peeking out amidst the rubble. What can we do?

The house speaks to me.

"I am in danger. The tides are rising, the storms more violent. Protect your land and me."

Our home is vulnerable to flooding, storm surges, hurricanes, high tides and wind damages now. Will the forces of nature take over? How much more land will wash away to sea? How much more damage can we sustain? Can we save the Blessed House?

CHAPTER 2
Divine Intervention

We were getting help from above—The Divine Spirits—even when we didn't know we needed it. The revelation began when our friend, Frank, said to my husband, "Tom, why don't you buy this car I'm selling and save me the money on advertising."

"We don't need a car Frank. We do need a larger house," he said. Frank countered back with,

"You want a house? I'll sell you a house, the Priest's house, the one next door to me. Tom was aghast! Although he had never seen the inside of the large house he knew the superb location on the water and immediately agreed to buy the house.

"How much do you want for it?" Tom asked. Frank set a price.

"Agreed?" said Tom as he and Frank shook hands. It was settled, all in a matter of fifteen minutes.

Tom came home and announced to me, "I bought us a house today, on the water, next door to Frank and Sue's. It was the Priest's house."

That's what everyone called the house, although Frank and Sue owned the former summer house since the priest died seven years ago. Frank installed a boiler for heat and rented it year-round to a family of Carnival people. I was overwhelmed by my husband's disclosure. I couldn't believe that Tom who procrastinates, investigates and deliberates before making minor decisions had made a very major one so quickly. I was thrilled that our life-long dream of living in a house on the water was materializing. Having more living space for our five teenagers and ten year old will make our lives more pleasurable. It wasn't until three days later that we both saw the house for the first time.

Driving down Buttonwoods Avenue we came to a fork in the road. In the middle is a triangle with a flowering tree and several multi-colored flowers. At the entrance to each road are two ten foot high circular fieldstone pillars. These sentries and a sign announce that you are entering Old Buttonwoods, a private compound. We enter on the right and drive down the narrow tree-lined, dead-end road. There is a hush and a coolness in the air.

We turn into a crushed broken-plates driveway and see the back of a three story sad square-box house. It is encased in a dirty-white and green ribbed slate covering. A run-down sloping cement garage listed on the end of the property behind the house. Walking around to the front of the house we are met with a spectacular 180 degree view of Greenwich Bay from high atop the hill. There is something about the seaside that is calming. The tired house vanished as this priceless view penetrated my eyes, ears, nose, mouth and skin. Several marinas, Goddard Park and Patience Island are vistas that dot this watery landscape. In the distance we can see the spires of the Jamestown and Newport bridges as they meet the cloudless azure sky. The hill is fifty feet of grass that slopes down to an inviting sandy beach. The low green scrub brush sprinkled with violet wild flowers separates the grass from the beach sand. Several white-masted sailboats are sailing comfortably in a light breeze toward the Greenwich Cove. The only sounds we can hear are the gentle waves humming a rhythmic tune. Several small power boats and one day-sailor boat are bobbing on their homemade moorings in front of our house. As I breathe in the salty-clean air and touch the clear rippling water with my fingertips, my soul fills up with peace and joy. I am home! This view is worth it. Now, let's go look inside the tired wrinkled-box house. We can always renovate!

Walking in the front door we are surrounded by tongue and groove knotty-pine walls and dark plywood ceilings creating the ambiance of a cozy seaside cottage.

"That's where Father St. Jean said Mass for his parishioners and neighbors. This was a chapel with an altar," said Frank pointing to a raised platform in the right hand corner of the living room. Later, an old kneeler was discovered in the garage. Frank was giving us a tour of the house. The living room and dining room were long and narrow lying side by side. At the end of the dining room was a small bedroom with an elaborate marble-backed sink.

"This was the priest's bedroom," continued Frank as he led us through the living room to a small kitchen. An adjoining lavette contained another lavish marble top sink. "Where does this door in the kitchen lead?" asked my husband.

"That's a back door leading to a small porch and the backyard," said Frank. As we ambled through the house a warm, safe feeling is growing inside me. It is almost as if the house is speaking to me.

Preserve the knotty pine walls!
Knock down the living/dining room wall!
Let the vibrant sunshine reflecting on the Bay waters in!
Put in many wide windows!
Place the dining room table where the altar stood!
Preserve the marble sinks!
Turn the kitchen into a library/office!
Fill it with books—a secluded room—a room for reading, a room
for healing—a room for clients!

Frank led us upstairs. There are four small knotty-pine, dark plywood ceiling guest bedrooms and one large bathroom. Each bedroom has a mirrored cedar closet. The house is speaking.

Add two more bedrooms!
Let the children design their own rooms!
Install new plumbing and two sinks in their bathroom!

The central corridor led us to a room which is narrow and extends the full width of the house. It is surrounded by windows on three sides. Frank explained, "This was a sun porch that the priest enclosed."

I look out at the awesome view of the Bay waters, shaded on one side by an enormous swamp maple tree and hear the house speaking to me again.

This will be a great master bedroom and sitting room! Enlarge it
and add a bathroom. This will be a pleasant place to meditate, and
pray, write and sleep!

The tour continued down to the lower level recreation room. We are greeted by a foot of water in this knotty-pine, walk-out room.

"I guess I'll have to install a sump pump." said Tom.

"I guess so," agreed Frank.

"What else is down here?"

"There is a boiler room and a second kitchen around the corner."

After the tour my husband and I agreed that this worn house has a lot of potential. Major renovations can bring it to life for our large family. We are enthused and full of hope. As I took one last look around, the house spoke once more.

This is a place of peace and calm and healing, this Priest's House!
The Spirits of those before you linger and bless all who come here!

"Step right up! Throw the plates! Break a plate and win a prize! Try your luck!" yelled the Carnival man at seaside Rocky Point Amusement Park in Warwick. The traveling Carnival man had a concession at Rocky Point, where people threw plates and tried to break them to win a prize during the summer and fall seasons. In the wintertime he traveled south to many more carnivals leaving his family in the rented Priest's house. Our neighbor Frank told us they are a quiet family who have three children who go to the neighborhood school. The husband, Mr. Carnival Man, did not like the dirt driveway so he took all the broken pieces of plates from his concession and spread them on the driveway. I thought it made a colorful driveway but I didn't like the crunch sounds when the tires made contact.

We bought the thirty-eight year old house in November 1976. We gave the tenants, the traveling Carnival man and his family, two months to move. January, February, March, April and now May—the Carnival people would not move. Anxious to begin renovations, my husband informed the family that we would begin construction one day in May 1977. A three man crew of workmen arrived and removed the roof off the kitchen in preparation of building two new bedrooms upstairs. In the middle of the night, the Carnival people stole away leaving behind many outdated Centennial Carnival dishes. "Canal Fulton, Ohio, Centennial Year 1904," I read on this stack of heavy green and white earthenware plates. In the middle of the plate there is a painting of several boats on the Canal Fulton waters. For many years I wondered about these plates. Where did they come from? Is there such a place? I stacked the plates, about fifty, away along with many mismatched colorful kitchen plates.

Use these plates on the porch in the summertime. They are
part of the ambiance of this casual house.

The house whispered to me.

Years later the mystery was revealed. I served dinner on these plates as I did every summer on my porch to my guests. This year my niece Kim and her family were visiting from Ohio.

"Canal Fulton," she exclaimed. "That's where we live in Ohio. My husband's family came from Canal Fulton."

"Is that the name of a town, Canal Fulton?" I asked.

"Yes, it's named after a famous Canal that runs through the middle of the town." When Tom and I visited Canal Fulton several years later for her brother's wedding we took a picture of the antique boats on the famous Canal Fulton.

Crash! Bang! The fragile upstairs windows shook and one fell and smashed on the ground below. It was Memorial Day. We always celebrated with our friends, the Daley family, in a park. The house speaks to me.

Bring your friends. Have a picnic on the huge jaded picnic table under the

*old swamp maple tree. Enjoy the shade, the grassy slope to the beach and
the southerly sea breezes.*

Our ten children ran around the beach and in and out of the empty
house with abandon, especially my youngest son, Dennis, and their Brian.
These two ten year olds had unstoppable energy. Through the
windowless window we recognized their yelps of "We didn't do it. We
didn't do anything." No one was hurt so we all had a good laugh as we
reinforced our plans to gut the house and rebuild from the inside out.

Before we move into the Blessed House we celebrate with food, family
and friends as the people who lived here before us did. I feel the spirits
must be guiding me.

CHAPTER 3
Rebuilding a House and a Family

Tom and I have a fine sturdy marriage of almost twenty years. We are devoted to each other and take our marriage vows seriously. We have homologous values; creating a family, raising them to love God and themselves, to be independent, caring and kind to others and to enjoy life's challenges and rewards.

Our greatest challenge now is to rebuild and renovate the Priest's House as a loving family project. We know what we want in a house. We want a large well-lighted great room with fireplace and dining table where we can have family gatherings, celebrations, graduations and entertaining. We want it to face south and overlook the water. We want a large screened-in porch for summertime lounging, reading, dining and entertaining. We want a recreation room with pool or ping-pong for our children and their friends. We want a garage and a cellar where the boys can tinker with cars and gadgets. We want a quiet study with bookcases, desk and comfortable chair for reading and so I can work at home. We want a private bedroom suite for Tom and I with a sitting room overlooking the water and a separate bathroom. We want four bedrooms for our six children, with their own two sink bathroom. We want a lavette on the first floor and a bathroom with shower in the recreation room for the beach goers. We want a spacious sunny, well-equipped kitchen where I can enjoy one of my many passions—cooking for family and friends. The Priest's House will work well for our family's needs.

After firing three sets of carpenters who showed up and worked intermittently for three months the Divine Spirits sent Steve, a first-class carpenter who worked alone and charged by the hour. This six foot four denim clad carpenter looked more like a movie star with his muscular physique and long wavy blonde hair. His energy and enthusiasm radiate like a ray of sunshine. He took us to his beautiful country home in the rural woods, that he built himself, to show us his skills. His artistic talents abounded from the rustic built-in kitchen and bathroom cabinets, coffee table, kitchen island, kitchen table and china closet. They are outstanding pieces for a showplace home. We are also overwhelmed by his massive floor-to-ceiling fireplace.

"Steve, do you think you can build some furniture for us?" I asked.

"Of course, what do you need?"

"A china closet, maybe a kitchen table and I would love to have a fireplace."

"Slow down, Barbara," my husband said. "Let Steve renovate the house first."

We feel God's blessings again. Steve captured the flavor of his rustic home complimenting his surroundings, the woods. We are convinced that he can transform the Priest's House into a viable family home for us in our surroundings, the Bay Waters.

Not everyone is pleased with our purchase, especially our children.

"Dad, what were you thinking when you bought this old house?"

"This is a rundown shack, the windows rattle and I don't want to live in it."

"You'd have to be a magician to make this place liveable," our teenagers voiced in unison. They cannot envision the potential. With promises of a spacious home that they could help design, five bedrooms, a recreation room, a two car garage and our own private beach we finally won them over. We agreed not to move in until the house was complete.

The renovation is a team effort, with Steve the Captain and Master Carpenter, Tom, the First Mate, our own General Contractor, myself and our six children are the Crew. We begin to tear down and build up this ship for launching together. Steve is a miracle worker encouraging the family's participation and showing endless patience with us novices. The children's devotion to the project is growing as they willingly participate within their fluctuating schedules of school, sports and part-time work. They contribute their ideas and creativity as well as their hard labor; choosing the color of their bedroom walls and carpets and lighting fixtures while straining their backs helping to pour and level the five car cement driveway. The family serves many functions.

Demolition Team

We tear down the old wooden ceilings and strip the walls to the shell in preparation for new insulation, electrical wiring, copper pipes and a plaster ceiling.

Architects

We design where new windows will go, select sliding glass doors for entrances, exits. We select sliding glass doors instead of porch windows.

Designers

We help turn the existing kitchen into a walnut paneled book-shelved library/office. We help in the change of the existing first floor bedroom into a sunny modern functional kitchen.

Engineers

Our thinking process takes precedent. The experts are consulted.

"Can we knock the wall down between the living room, dining room and chapel so we can have one large room with a sweeping view of the water?"

"Yes," they say, "but it takes a lot of hard work." We help to knock the walls down, eliminate the altar platform and install a twenty-eight foot supporting steel beam across the width of the ceiling. Eventually the steel beam is covered in knotty pine to match an existing beam that hides pipes.

"We ran out of knotty pine. We need about ten more feet. Does anyone know where we can get it?" asked Steve.

The original honey colored knotty pine walls had been carefully dismantled one board at a time. When the new insulation etc. was placed inside, each board was replaced on the walls in the new configuration minus ten feet. My husband Tom's boss gave him some holey old authentic barn board taken from a country barn in Burrillville. Steve's eyes lit up when he saw the barn board. Carpenter's magic—he installed pieces on the fireplace wall blending in with the knotty pine; he nailed barn board on all the porch walls and with the remaining barn board he created a kitchen trestle table that is used everyday.

Plumbers

Under the guidance of my father, a Master plumber, we pull out old bathroom and kitchen fixtures, solder pipes, design new places for lavatory fixtures and installation for three bathrooms and a lavette.

Carpenters

We assisted the carpenter building bathroom cabinets, window frames and walls. We helped to shingle the outside of the house with weathered shingles.

Painters

We helped to stain and varnish thirty doors, twenty-six window frames, a floor-to-ceiling bookcase cabinet and bathroom cabinets. We paint the trim, in the house, out of the house and on the garage.

Clean Up Crew

We are most valuable as a clean-up crew. Everyday there is debris that we shovel and carry out to the truck and haul away to the dump. We clean up on our own and we are good at it. We are handy men willing and able to function in whatever capacity we are needed. The continuous blessings from the Divine Spirits strengthen the bond in our family physically and spiritually, with love, as we enthusiastically labor together for seven months.

Family Team

Most of all we are a family team working together to build our dream home where we will live comfortably with each other. We are building a home where our children will be happy to bring friends, spouses and grandchildren. We are joined together spiritually as a family forever.

Heating Up the Family

Build a fireplace so the family will feel the warmth
of a roaring fire in their body and their souls.

I listen as the house speaks to me. Looking at this huge heap of assorted rocks in the middle of the unfinished great room floor I try to visualize them as a fireplace and indoor grille.

"Steve, I would really like to have a fireplace in this room. It will compliment the knotty pine and be so relaxing in our cold New England winters," I said to our carpenter.

"This floor won't support a heavy fireplace. If you really want it I'll have to buttress the foundation in the cellar. I can do it," he replied.

"Great," my husband and I chorused.

"I saw a built-in gas grille in a house and was fascinated with it. Imagine cooking on the grille all year long! Do you think that's possible Steve?" asked my husband.

"Well, I'd have to see the unit but I bet I could make a well and make it fit. If we put it on this wall we can have double doors with one door opening into this room and the other door opening on the porch for summertime. We probably can vent it through the porch roof."

"That sounds fantastic," we agreed.

"What will you use? I really like the old rocks in your fireplace.

"We can do it together," reassured Steve.

Thus we began a unique extraordinary family adventure.

"I'll build the fireplace and grille if you gather the rocks by dismantling the stone walls on my property in the woods. I have miles of rock walls. You also have to transport them to your house."

The stones are a gift from Steve to us.

On a Saturday morning at 6:00 a.m. in mid-February we are squeezed together with our four boys into the cab of an archaic rickety borrowed dump truck. This lone arduous crowded drive with no heat, on one-lane country roads is making us cranky. On arrival Steve and his wife treat us to a mouth-watering breakfast of ham, eggs, coffee, homemade cornbread and homemade jam. The fire in his enormous fireplace, delicious food and gracious hospitality awaken our bodies and our spirits as we prepare for our back-breaking task. Outside we are awed by the quiet and the beauty of his many-acred snow-laden land surrounded by meandering old-fashioned rock walls. Fortified with food we brave the 30 degree weather walking through the snow, collecting the heavy rocks and heaving them up into the dump truck. This is work for strong muscular men we soon find out.

"Dad, it's a good thing you brought us along. You could not have done this without us," said our son Steve.

"Yeah, Dad, this is hard work. It's not for wimps. It's a good thing we left the girls at home. Not you, Mom, you're helping," joined Mike. We do not quit, even now that the snowflakes are coming down and we can no longer see or feel our frozen gloved fingers.

"Just think, Mom, we'll be able to sit in front of a warm fire eating hamburgers in January. We'd better keep going." Dennis, the other cheerleader is spurring us on. We labor all day and when we arrive home we labor more as we empty the stones one by one from the truck onto our front lawn, careful not to break them.

"We did it!" shouted Tommy. The fun and camaraderie my 'men' and I are enjoying offsets our aching bones making this a day to remember in the enchanting peaceful woods. The real work begins with Steve building a foundation in the cellar. When completed, I am astonished at the precise selection process he gives the rocks from the pile in the middle of the floor. They all look alike to me. Steve points out their different sizes, large, medium and small, and their shapes, round, flat and oblong. Upon looking closer I see many shades of gray and a few that are sparkling white. In subsequent weeks Steve fulfilled our expectations with a superb stone and mortar fireplace that reaches to the ceiling. A heatalator is added to throw more warmth into the room. The gas grille is built into the fireplace and can be used indoors in winter and outdoors on the porch in the summertime.

Eating our gourmet hamburgers and cuddling up around the cozy warm fire in the fireplace we all helped to build, we are reminded that this is a special place where love abounds.

The Table

In the midst of all these renovations we acquire the most significant piece of furniture we ever owned.

"Barbara, my boss has a large oak conference table he said we can have but we have to take it now. He needs the space," said my husband.

"It's a beautiful antique. I don't know where we can store it until we're ready. I hate to miss this opportunity," he continued.

"That's wonderful, Tom, just what we need. Take it. We'll figure it out when it comes," I replied.

The only place the eight foot long, four foot wide table fit is in the dusty dirty plaster and paint splattered great room of our unfinished house. Setting among the paint cans, flaking plaster, dripping varnish, mortar and rocks and endless sawdust the Table becomes a workbench and lunch table for all of us construction workers. I continually reapply many sheets of plastic to protect our valuable acquisition.

With construction finished I hear the house speaking to me.

Leave the table in this place where the sacred altar once stood
and the Priest changed the bread and wine into the body and
blood of Christ. You can bring many to your table of plenty.

Our magnificent honey colored striated oak wood grained table with four large round pedestal legs holding it will play a principal role in our future.

Moving Day Detour

We finish transforming the Priest's impoverished summer house into a grand comfortable home by the sea in February 1978. Moving Day is scheduled. Snow begins to fall. We are all caught off guard. A Northeast Blizzard blankets the State of R.I. with four feet of snow. The State is paralyzed and people are stranded for three days. Cars are stalled and abandoned on every highway. No one moved except by foot, sled or skimobile. My husband slept in his office in Providence, as did several hundred office workers. Our carpenter is grounded with my six children and me in our ranch house after stalling his truck on the highway. Shoveling ourselves out the next day we are enveloped in an alien silence and blinded by snow-white sunshine. The snow plows do not come for three days. We take turns walking to the grocery store for bread and milk.

Two weeks later when plowing, towing and shoveling open the roads again, we make the most remarkable and anticipated move in our lives to our seaside home.

As each family member moves in to our new surroundings, we are satisfied and content with our Blessed House. The family settles into the house like a baby drinking his mother's milk. Michael, our oldest son, a serious accounting student at Providence College now, is pleased to have his own bedroom.

Steven, a senior in high school likes his separate room also and is particularly looking forward to satisfying his mechanical curiosity and his many projects in our new oversized garage. The garage was one of the astonishing feats that the carpenter and my men; four sons and husband, accomplished. Our old garage had to be demolished. More blessings came our way. Our friend, Dick, did not need his office's three car garage in Pawtucket. He gave it to us and all we had to do was disassemble the large structure piece by piece intact, load the pieces onto a flat bed truck and transport it twenty miles to Warwick. Then, they began the tedious job of assembling all the pieces and constructing a separate two-car garage. What skills my men learned from this monumental year long job as they nailed joists together, assembled walls, tarred and shingled the roof and poured the cement floor and driveway. This was first rate fun for the boys.

Cathleen, our oldest child, a college sophomore teacher-education student shared a new bedroom with her sister, Susan, a freshman in high school. Cathleen's creative talents decorated their room; she sewed peach drapes and patchwork quilts for their twin beds. The turquoise patterned king-size quilt and pillow shams she sewed for our master bedroom blended well with the turquoise carpet reflecting the sea outside our windows.

The children's enthusiasm caught on fire when they selected rug colors, wall colors and lamps for their individual rooms. The youngest boys, Tommy and Dennis, share the other new bedroom across the hall. Blue walls and blue rug suited Tommy, an eighth grader. The built-in shelves are ideal for closeting Dennis's 'treasures'.

The teenagers have room to entertain their friends, indoors and outdoors. The tension we felt in our cramped ranch house has dissipated as each family member has their own private space as well as many communal areas. Every morning I look out my bedroom window, count my blessings and thank the Lord for all He has given me.

The house seems to say to me.
Pray, Meditate, Rest, Write,
Be close to the Lord.

I was thirsty and you gave me drink.

CHAPTER 4
The Party House

Bang! Ka Boom! Hiss! The thunderous fireworks are punching multi-colored light holes in the black sky over the calm waters of Greenwich Bay. Assembled on the grassy bank in front of our house, looking at this spectacular 4th of July display, are three generations of family and many friends of Tom, Dick and Jack. This visual feast continues on our semi-circular Bay which is dotted with crackling, leaping, red-orange flames from several bonfires along the shore line. Fireworks, Friendships, Food and Fun are abundant and flourishing.

This festive celebration is being held at Tom's and my home in honor of our first-born child,

Cathleen's birthday. We have been gathering here on the eve of July 4th since we bought this large old house in 1976. Our three families, the Malones, Murphys and Daleys, have spent many hours together. Between us we have fifteen children, twenty grandchildren and many spouses—all are present this year. This is our biggest annual celebration—sixty-five people on our front lawn.

Rounding up all the children who are present for a 4th of July picture is a highlight of the party. They are assembled on the 5 stairs of the deck at the front of the house. Each year the number of smiling faces increases and the latest picture is displayed in a prominent place in the Blessed House.

The Lord has blessed us with many cherished lasting friends. Tom, Dick and Jack have known each other since the first and second grade at St. Michael's School. They grew up in a close community that revolved around their Church, School and Sports. Jack and Dick were honorable students but Tom's halo would dip sometimes. In school he frequently had his knuckles rapped on with a ruler by his strict nun-teacher for misbehavior. As an altar boy, when he left Church one weekday morning with his cassock over his arm, the smell of fresh baked apple pies on the window at the hospital was too much to resist. He followed some friends who tucked the pies under their cassocks and later they devoured them.

They lived for their sports. Pick-up games, baseball, football, basketball; whatever the season they would show up at the school or playground and imitate their sports heroes. Dick excelled in baseball and Tom in football, continuing to play in high school. Jack played ball occasionally but mostly cheered on the sidelines. He wasn't allowed to get dirty. The trio studied together at LaSalle High School and later Providence College. Dick went on to Medical School and became a distinguished orthopedic surgeon. Tom attended Law school and became a successful businessman. Jack became an eminent teacher and assistant principal in the Providence School System.

At a Providence College Prom, Helen, Carole and I, their future wives, were surprised to find that we knew each other. We all attended St. Mary's Bayview High School together. Helen and I graduating together and

Carole following us two years later. Our unconditional love and friendship has flourished for the past fifty-two years. In the early years our fifteen children swam, ate and played together at Bonnet Shores Beach all summer long. They formed friendships that have lasted into their adulthood. The Malone, Murphy, Daley clan all gathers for a family portrait at each of our children's weddings. Now, we welcome the arrival of more grandchildren.

One day when my granddaughter was five years old, she saw me putting on the party tablecloth and asked,

"Grandma, why do we have a party every time we come to your house?" Her brother Sean, who is two years older, immediately replied,

"Emily, don't you know, this is the Party House." So it seems!

When we renovated we added a thirty foot porch that runs the length of the house. Entering our house from the driveway leads you onto our three-season porch.

Welcome to the Beach

A seashell sign and large furry red lobster on the wall greet you. You are surrounded by five sliding glass doors, one leading into the living room, the other four to the wrap-around deck, taking advantage of the view. The rugged beauty of the other wall, which is from an old barn shows the scars, nail holes and patina that comes with age. A vivid multi-colored fish mobile hangs amid many flowering plants. The cozy slip-covered cushioned wicker couches and chairs are at one end of this long porch. The guests settle into these comfortable cushioned couches and chairs looking at the panoramic view of the Bay or having lively conversations about their recent ventures. Also popular are the rocking chairs. They are everywhere; on the porch, the deck, in the great room. I use one to sit in when I counsel clients in the library/office. Two chairs are gifts, one from my sister in Ohio and one from Tom's buddies on his sixtieth birthday. Rocking chairs are a staple in a home on the water.

A tile-top table and several chairs anchor the other end of the porch. The table is always laden with appetizing food depending on the occasion. On the one solid wall is a large map of Narragansett and Greenwich Bays pinpointing—You are Here!

This is where all the socializing begins—a bar, a built-in gas grille, a refrigerator and a buffet built by my brother as office furniture, full of Carnival dishes, silverware and glasses make entertaining so easy. Beach towels, suntan lotion, bug spray and many summer hats sit atop one end of the buffet.

One year my son Tommy had a surprise birthday party for his wife, Lori, and multiple colorful lanterns, streamers and Hawaiian leis were put up as decoration. They are now part of the permanent decor along with the blinking lighted 4th of July flag in the window and a recent addition of a seven foot lighted palm tree, a gift from our daughter Susan. The mood is always set and our house is always ready.

We have been having family parties, extended family parties and friends parties since we moved into our house. Our first party was an Open House where a sacred blessing was bestowed on us all by Father Keough. We have been sharing our love and joy ever since.

When my Italian genes surge I love to cook. My specialties are Lasagna, Meatballs, Sausage and Pasta and Linguini and Clams. The latter I dig with my clam rake in the shallow water in front of our house. People love to eat good food and we love to entertain. My husband amuses our guests with his illustrious wit and sense of humor. We celebrate birthdays, holidays, marriages, anniversaries, graduations, Camp Grandma and family reunions all year long. Sometimes we celebrate for no reason. We always enjoy the love, friendship, fun and good food at our Blessed Party House, my special place.

Party Cheesecake

My family enjoys a sweet after dinner almost as much as pasta. I use my Aunt Anna's Best Ever Cheesecake as a base and blend it into my own Party Cheesecake.

Crust
1 3/4 cup fine graham cracker crumbs
1/4 cup finely chopped walnuts
½ tsp. Cinnamon
1/4 lb. melted butter or margarine

Grease 10 inch spring form pan.
Combine all ingredients.
Press all but 3 tsp. of mixture on bottom and sides of pan.

Filling
3 eggs, well beaten
1 cup sugar
1/4 tsp. Salt
2 tsp. Vanilla
2—8 oz. packages cream cheese
1 lb. Ricotta cheese
2 cups sour cream

Beat together eggs, sugar, salt, vanilla and cream cheese.

Add ricotta cheese and beat until smooth.

Fold in sour cream—do not beat sour cream.

Pour into graham cracker crust.

Sprinkle remaining crust mixture on top of filling.

Bake in 375 degree oven for 50 minutes.

Filling will be a little soft when done.

Cool and refrigerate.

CHAPTER 5
Quahogging in my Front Yard

"Drop it! Did you hear me? I said drop the clams!" he shouted. I was momentarily stunned and did not react immediately. I had just finished raking, digging and gathering quahogs and was about to carry my booty home when my peaceful afternoon was abruptly interrupted. I looked up at this bellowing intruder and saw a big brown bear of a man atop the cliff next to my house on Greenwich Bay. My mind and my eyes were having difficulty coordinating this spectacle. Shattering my serenity and replacing it with anxiety, I stared at this brown uniformed police officer who had his right hand on his hip-holstered gun. How could this be happening? I am not a criminal. I am a harmless woman quahogging at our isolated private Buttonwoods Beach. Steve did not warn me about this! What am I supposed to do now. This wasn't in your instruction manual, Steve. Steve our Swedish carpenter, taught me many carpentry skills as well as—How to Quahog.

One day in the midst of my staining twenty-six doors while Steve built floor to ceiling bookcases in our new library-office room, I looked out the window and saw a few people quahogging in front of the house.

"I would love to quahog. I wish I knew how to do it," I said to Steve. "Really? I can teach you. I've been quahogging for years but finish up that door first or you will end up with two shades of stain," he answered.

He had a quahog rake in his truck among his tools. We searched for a pail and headed off to the beach leaving our unfinished work behind.

1. Raking the Clams

"Before we begin you need to know about clams. There are two types—soft clams and hard clams or quahog clams. The quahogs are plentiful in the Bay." he began. "Isn't that what I use to make chowder or linguini and clams?" I asked. "Yes," he replied. "Hopefully we will find a few soft clams, like littlenecks, which are small and cherrystones which are medium. You can steam the soft littlenecks which have the necks hanging out. They are delicious dipped in melted butter."

"How about the cherrystones? What do I do with them?" I asked. "You can eat them uncooked, grill them or add them whole to linguini. They are very tasty. One more thing, make sure they are alive-tightly closed shells."

"Let's go Steve, I can't wait to begin!"

I watched intently as Steve instructed,

"Begin by raking the surface of the soft sandy bottom gently with a quahog rake at low tide.

I prefer a wide-toothed long handle rake but you can use one with a basket connected to it. When you hear the rake go 'Klink', you immediately dig down at that spot, with force on your rake. You have to dig quickly in the obscure waters because the quahog feels the rake and instantly burrows deeper and deeper into the dirt."

Now, it was my turn to rake.

"Gently, go gently," he admonished me. "You're going to scare the quahogs away!"

Eventually I was able to get the right cadence and was thrilled when I heard the 'Klink'. When I tried to capture the quahog in my rake and bring it to the surface I was not as successful. I brought up mud as the "klinked." quahogs eluded me.

"Barbara, you have to be faster," said Steve.

I persisted but found more mastery by dropping the rake after the 'Klink' and digging in the black mud with my bare hands.

"I got it! I got it, a big beautiful quahog Steve," I shrieked.

"Alright, I guess, whatever works for you. Now wash the mud off the quahog in the salty water before you put it in the bucket. It's best to have a floating basket surrounded by an inner tube or even a potato sack secured to your waist with a rope," he said.

We continued quahogging and my excitement mounted as I saw our pile of quahogs filling the large pail. I feel like a miner who has panned gold. Exuberant! I feel I am getting Help from Above.

2. Cleaning and Opening the Clams

"We have more work to do before you can cook the clams, Barbara." said Steve. "What's next?" I asked eagerly. "Put the clams in a pail of salt water from the Bay for a few hours and they will cleanse themselves by spitting into the pail. Never use fresh water or they will drown," he warned.

I was amused watching the clams spitting black flecks into the clean salty water. Steve continued his instructions,

"We have to put the clams in the refrigerator for an hour or two before we open them up."

"Why, Steve?" I inquired.

"The quahogs will go to sleep in the cold and they will be easier to open. In the meantime, we'll get ready. Place some newspapers on the picnic table and get a knife and two bowls. It's best to use a clam knife which is rounded and smooth or a clam shucker which is quicker."

"Shall I get the clams now?" I asked.

"Gently take them out of the refrigerator so they won't wake up."

Just then my husband arrived from work. I was so glad that he could learn how to open the clams. I loved digging them up but I wasn't so sure about this next step. Tom's interest peaked when I told him I would cook linguini and clams and stuffed quahogs, although I had never made these recipes. He immediately dove into the project. I assembled the tranquil quahogs calmly on the picnic table. We watched as Steve slowly stood the quahog on end and placed the knife between the center crack. With one swift downward push he opened the clam cutting through the tough muscle. When the clam was open he carefully saved the juice in one bowl.

He resumed, "See this small area of brownish green, that's the stomach and you need to remove it as it doesn't taste good. Cut it out with the knife and throw it away."—second bowl.

"Now, cut out the quahog and place it in the bowl with the clam juice," said Steve as we took turns opening the clams. I found it difficult. Tom and Steve were doing well until a quahog came along that would not open.

"When you have a resistant muscle, if you tap the knife with a hammer, it will open."

When I was cleaning up I put aside some empty shells to make stuffed quahogs or stuffies. Now, all I have to do is realize my quahog cooking skills. I will forever be grateful to Steve, a messenger sent to us when we needed him who taught us all so much. But, he didn't tell me about the Environmental Police.

The Police officer bellowed louder, "Drop the quahogs."

I finally dropped the quahogs while my glaring eyes rested on his gun and my heart thumped louder.

"The Bay is closed due to heavy rains earlier in the week. This is a warning! Next time you'll pay a hefty fine," he said sternly as he watched me closely. I reluctantly emptied my sack of gold that took me two hours to gather. My heart sank along with the laboriously dug quahogs. I should have known that the Bay closes when we have sustained rain due to run-offs in Providence. I was bewitched by the sunshine, warm low-tide waters and quahogs that beckoned to me. I slithered off down the beach and up the hill to my house under the austere gaze of the stately Environmental Police officer.

This defeat did not discourage me through the years. I continued to perfect my clamming skills with the help of my summertime neighbor and friend, Norm. He has summered on this Bay since he was a child and knew all the nuances of clamming. Whenever the beguiling sunshine and low tides appeared, Norm and I would venture into the clam-filled shallow waters. We were a team now and I was delighted. When the supply of clams lessened through the years I became more dependent on my clamming partner. Norm could go places that I would not go—deep waters, up to his neck. That's where the untouched clams were hiding and his expertise and his special rake given to him by his grandfather allowed him to clam without drowning in deep water. I was a low-tide partner who frequently dug one, two, sometimes three clams in our two-hour sojourn. Norm's generous spirit filled our quahog bucket and no one knew otherwise. I volunteered to cook Linguini and Clams and Garlic bread at my house. His wife, Marge, my husband and several friends joined us in these united quahog feasts.

One year while I was in the kitchen cooking and Norm was supervising/helping me, my guests were very quiet. We walked softly onto the porch and heard Norm's wife, Marge, reading out loud from her latest novel. My guests were mesmerized by this would-be-author's vivid descriptions of lust in the afternoon with her sex-driven characters. Marge entertained everyone until dinner was served.

Many of my friends said they wish they could quahog. This Sunday afternoon I invited our friends to come quahogging with me.

Quahog Party
2:00 P.M.—Learn to Quahog
5:00 P.M.—Enjoy The Quahog Feast

The conditions are ideal for quahogging; a light breeze blowing, the sun shining and moon-low-tide waters. Very few guests arrived at two to rake, gather, and prepare the quahogs. Most of my friends arrived in time for the Stuffed Clam hors d'ouves and drinks. Oh, well, it seemed like a good idea at the time.

"Barbara, can I bring my Cambodian students to an outing at your house and you can teach them to quahog?" asked my friend, Karon, who is Director of a school that teaches English and Career Skills to adult refugees and immigrants.

"Yes, I'm thrilled to have enthusiastic students," I replied.

This second group of disciples, fifteen Cambodian refugee women who spoke limited English were eager to learn. I was one of their teachers and had heard their tragic stories of their homeland and their journey to America. In the classroom I listened to the pain in their lives. I am delighted to introduce some fun. I collected as many quahog rakes as I could from my neighbors. The women were like little children gleefully playing in the sandbox. When we ran out of rakes, I taught them how to twist their bare heel around in the sandy waters until they felt something hard and dig it up with their hands. When they tired they sat on the deck of the house eating their prepared lunch of rice, fish and vegetables they brought with them. What a fun-filled afternoon! There were more quahogs in the Bay than usual that day and everyone was able to take some home to cook for their families. The spirits before me were here again with us today. The Cambodian women recalled this joyous memory of quahogging in the Bay in front of my house, during their graduation ceremony.

I never know who my friend Karon will bring to the Blessed House. We always welcome them even on short notice. One time she brought a group of Russian refugees who are settling in R.I. Another time, a group of Latvian business men visiting the U.S. on an educational visa. Meandering on the front lawn with food and drink, my family is receiving 'our education' from these distinguished limited-English visitors.

Through the years I practiced, experimented and perfected my quahog recipes. The joy I feel in my heart every time I pick up my rake and tubed-basket on a sunny low-tide day is almost as great as the pleasure I receive when I serve my family and friends.

"Grandma, look, I've got a quahog. I got one. I dig deep with my hands. This one is squiggly." squealed my grandson. Digging clams with my grandchildren is like having a slice of Heaven on this earth.

Sometimes when my body is digging for the succulent clams, my mind is digging for life's mysteries.

How do I fit into God's Divine Plan? What is the meaning of Life? What is my greatest gift? How can I share it? What is true love? I toss around these answers—Giving of myself, using my gifts, preparing fresh food for family and friends.

The blessedness I feel deep inside me comes directly from the people who were here before me, raking, cooking and serving as I am still doing.

3. Cooking the Quahogs

I use about twenty-five large quahogs for the following recipes, which yields about 1 quart of meat. Put the separated quahogs into a food processor and chop. The quahog juice is separate. Continue with the recipes on the following page.

Barbara's Linguini with White Clam Sauce

1 ½ lbs. linguini pasta

2 tablespoons olive oil

8 cloves garlic, minced

1 large onion, chopped

1 quart chopped clams or 25 large quahog meat

1 pint clam juice

1/3 cup chopped fresh parsley or 2 tablespoons dried parsley

½ cup white wine

1 teaspoon dried basil leaves

Ground black pepper to taste

Cook linguini.

Combine olive oil, garlic and onion.

Simmer until soft.

Stir in clam juice, parsley, wine, basil and pepper.

Simmer 10 minutes.

Stir in clams. I also add a few unopened cherrystone clams.
Simmer until clams open, about 2-3 minutes.

Serve over hot cooked linguini leaving the open cherrystone clams in the shell as garnish.

Garlic Bread

I always serve Garlic Bread with Linguini and Clams.

1 large loaf of Sicilian bread or other hard crusty Italian bread
Split the loaf in half lengthwise.

Combine 5-6 minced garlic cloves with extra virgin olive oil or 1 stick of margarine.
Melt in microwave.
Brush this mixture liberally on the opened bread.
Place under broiler a few minutes.
Put the 2 halves together and slice diagonally.
Serve warm.
I am inspired by the spirits to quahog, cook and feed family and friends. I want to share our celestial surroundings. The house speaks to me.

Continue to cook and feed your family and friends. Bring peace to your clients in their time of need,

Chapter 6
Old Buttonwoods

Religion by the Sea

"I now pronounce you husband and wife. May I present for the first time, Mr. & Mrs. Thomas Malone, III."

The minister's words rang in my ears at the wedding ceremony of our son Tom and his lovely bride Lorianne. We were in the Buttonwoods Beach Chapel, the corner stone of our special Old Buttonwoods community. What a feeling of reverence I felt knowing that this historic Queen Ann Colonial Revival Style Chapel has been in existence for one hundred and thirty years. How many weddings and other religious services have been held on this altar that is framed by a lavish stained glass window? A Baby Grand piano sits to the right of the altar. We watch Tom and his bride walk down the short aisle smiling at the full house of seventy-five family and friends who are sitting in the original small antique chairs of cane and mahogany.

In 1871, Old Buttonwoods was developed by Rev. Moses Bixby as a

Baptist religious retreat to bring together families dedicated to the worship of God. He intended that this seaside community, a 127 acre peninsula, be established for summer relaxation and prayer.

On this perfect cloudless September morning the wedding party is greeting guests in a reception line that snakes around the blue hydrangeas and manicured lawn in front of the chapel. I glance around at the surrounding cottages with their Victorian gingerbread trim and wrap-around porches. This architectural heritage of the past, the chapel and two hundred summer houses built from 1871 to 1915 were modeled after Oak Bluffs on Martha's Vineyard. I marvel that the same houses, now converted to year-round use, are still standing on the narrow streets shaded by tall Buttonwood trees leading to private beaches.

The only wide street, Beach Park Avenue, used to be a trolley turnaround when the trolleys carried people to the beach from the city. Another stop on the trolley line was the Buttonwoods Inn, a waterfront vacation resort for city goers, later converted to a nursing home and now a private residence.

What we value today is the feeling of being part of a community with old-fashion values. Everyone cares about their neighbors; the children, the elderly, the sick and those who are grieving a loss. Father Bixby's spirit lives on in the people of Old Buttonwoods.

Leaving the now non-denominational Chapel we drive through our private compound and pass the clay tennis courts, the baseball field and the Casino.

"Lori, this Casino is our community center. It has a large reception hall, bowling alleys and a stage. Your husband Tom used to bowl in the alleys. There are recreational programs for children and tennis lessons in the summer," I said.

"Were you a good bowler?" she asked Tom. "Of course I was, I still am. Mom, don't you and Dad go to dances in the Casino?"

"Oh yes, dances, meetings, cocktail parties, ham & bean dinners. You can even rent the hall for private parties," I answered. 'Do you know the Casino and the Chapel are on the National Register of Historic Places?" I asked.

"Maybe that makes ours a historic wedding," said Tom.

When we reached our destination, our home in this seaside community, we breathed in the salty air and felt the warm winds rustle our gowns and hair. The photographer captured the joy and love on the faces of the bride and groom with the whitecaps on the choppy waters of Greenwich Bay in the background. He also captured the sudden sharp gusts of wind that whipped my kinky hair into a 'Phyllis Diller' hairdo in the family wedding portrait. Oh my! Later that day the wedding party and guests roamed the house, porch, deck and lawn celebrating this joyous occasion.

The Buttonwoods Community was founded to serve and strengthen a special bond of family, friends and God by Rev. Bixby in 1871. Our home, built in 1939 by Father St. Jean and his parishioners, repeats this tradition sixty-eight years later. Father St. Jean established and built our home as a summer religious retreat to bring together families to worship God and enjoy seaside relaxation. An altar with kneelers and an adjacent dining room table were central to this summer retreat.

As we gather around our large dining room table toasting the bride and groom my thoughts are on the past. Here we are sitting at this table where the chapel and altar once stood. Many blessings have been bestowed on us in this house, families nurtured, friendships prospered and our faith strengthened and shared. We continue to cook, clam, feed, counsel and listen to people as we carry on the tradition in Old Buttonwoods of Rev. Bixby and Rev. St. Jean in this Blessed House.

Italian Wedding Soup

or

Escarole Chicken Soup

I call this a Holiday soup because I serve it as a first course at many Holiday dinners.

Boil 2-3 lbs. Escarole.

Cut into small pieces and set aside.

Take 1 lb. lean hamburg. Form into bite-size meatballs and set aside.

In a large 8-10 qt. pan place the following:

1 lg. 48 oz. can College Inn or similar chicken broth.

Refill the can with water 2 times and add to pot.

1 whole chicken, cut in pieces.

1 large onion, cut up.

3-4 carrots, cut up.

3 stalks celery, cut up.

2-3 cloves garlic, crushed.

Salt and pepper.

Simmer for about 2 hours.

Strain the soup and cut up chicken into small pieces and return chicken and vegetables to the pan.

Add meatballs, escarole and 1/4 box of Pastina Pasta to soup.

Cook until pasta is done.

I was a stranger and you welcomed me.

CHAPTER 7
Barbarella's Meatballs

"That's my meatball. Don't take my meatball," cried out my 2 ½ year old son Dennis to our esteemed dinner guest. The astonished guest, our parish priest, immediately dropped the meatball back into the mountainous bowl of meatballs as my youngest son scooped it onto his plate.

I was blessed with two Italian grandmothers who cooked delicious meatballs and dished it out with large spoonfuls of love. Both grandmothers were short, round and soft especially when they enveloped me in a hug of greeting. Ferdinandina, or Katie, as she called herself, was born on Federal Hill, in the city, an Italian enclave. My grandfather Giro, her husband, emigrated from The Isle of Ischia in Southern Italy where he was a sea captain. My other grandparents, Angelina and Rocco, also emigrated from Southern Italy in the mountains of Savoia di Lucania. They lived on a farm in North Providence.

I can still hear Angelina's sweet voice greeting me,

"Bar-ba-rella," lingering on the last syllable. It is Sunday afternoon and

Grandma is serving and cooking dinner for her 10 children, spouses and numerous grandchildren. The smells of garlic, tomato sauce, homemade sausage, spaghetti and a wood fire exhilarate my senses. There are two large, round dining room tables and a huge black wood stove in the oversized kitchen in the cellar of her home. We ate in shifts, all afternoon; antipasto, meatballs and spaghetti, zucchini and tomatoes, eggplant Parmesan, peppers, onions and sausages, fruit, cheeses, pies and coffee. After dinner the children wandered off to the couches to play Button, Button, Who's Got the Button or outdoors to play Hide and Seek in the barn and vineyard if it was good weather. Angelina died before I was old enough to get her food recipes but I inherited something more valuable—the recipe for life.

I wanted to capture that blissful feeling by cooking my own meatballs and homemade garlic tomato sauce for my husband and children. I wanted to share the joy and love I felt in my Grandmother's kitchen. So I sought out Grandma Katie, my mother's mother. Her kitchen was modern but the ambience was the same; fragrant smells of garlic, warm hugs and sharing platters of Italian food. "Manga, Manga," Eat, eat, "It's good for you." was her refrain. Our many hours of cooking lessons were mixed with sharing our joys and heartaches in life. Katie's recipes included hopes for my future and heartfelt forgiveness of others.

One day my three year old grandson Sean was packing his PJ's in his toy car and driving around his playroom. His mother asked him where he was going.

"I'm going to Grandma's house to get some meatballs!"

As mother, grandmother and hostess I serve everyone who comes to the Blessed House meatballs, spaghetti and homemade garlic tomato sauce on our large dining room table. The recipe is not magic but the love and sharing that is ladled out with every meatball is priceless.

I saw a cartoon that said that the world's greatest scholar and philosopher has been searching all his life for the universal secret of happiness. The wise man finally discovers the secret; not career success, not accumulating great wealth or winning enduring fame—It's meatballs and spaghetti! This will be my legacy, my beloved signature dish— Barbarella's Meatballs.

2 lbs. of Love

1 lb. of Family Values

Mix together with generous amounts of Sharing

Simmer with Happiness

Barbarella's Meatballs and Tomato Sauce

The most important ingredient in an Italian kitchen is homemade tomato sauce.

3 Tbsp. extra virgin olive oil

3—29 oz. cans tomato sauce

2—29 oz. can tomato puree

1—29 oz. can crushed tomatoes

1 small can tomato paste.

Mix above ingredients together in large pan.

Add, 6 to 8 cloves fresh garlic, crushed

2 bay leafs

fresh basil, chopped or 3-4 dry shakes

fresh parsley, chopped or 3-4 dry shakes

fresh oregano, or optional dry, 1-2 shakes

Stir ingredients together.

Add, sweet Italian sausage—1 lb.

hot Italian sausage—1 lb.

dry pepperoni—1 stick

Cook on simmer for 3 hours, stirring frequently.

Meatballs

The secret to tasty meatballs is to cook them in the homemade tomato sauce during the last hour of cooking the sauce.

Lean ground beef—3 lbs.

2 large eggs

basil and parsley —1 or 2 shakes

Italian bread crumbs or I make my own bread crumbs. I use stale Italian bread or crusty toast, and mix in food processor.

Mix bread crumbs with other ingredients to form firm balls. Drop right into simmering tomato sauce and cook one hour.

Book II

Healing Powers of Our House

I was ill and you cared for me.

CHAPTER 8
The Angel On My Shoulder

My Mother and Me

"My mother died last night." I proclaimed dispassionately to my group at the psychiatric hospital where I worked. Silence. Then,

"Are you alright?" asked the Social Worker.

"Yes." We continued to discuss our roles, our problems and concerns for the patients; the Psychiatrist, the Psychologist, the M.D. Coordinator, the Head Nurse, Staff Nurse and me, the Nurse Drama Therapist. We are a select group and I feel privileged to be a part of it. Our mission is to show how to be more effective with the patient's therapy by revealing our own fears and feelings in a safe group setting. No one ever did, including me. I surprised myself when I blurted out, "My mother died last night."

My healing had been going on for years in the Blessed House. Surrounded by a loving family, my past demons grew less and less fierce. My break-through came when I was forty years old but my abiding healing meandered and lingered through the years.

My mother stole away one afternoon when I was eight years old. She left my father, my four year old sister and six month old brother while my grandmother was babysitting. No one knew where she was for ten years. The Lord sent an Angel on my shoulder to help heal my broken heart. Her medicine was love doled out throughout my life, a spoonful at a time. The first spoonful is loving grandparents who cared for me when they could. The next dose of medicine is given by the caring nuns when I attended boarding school. The largest dose is given by my husband. I'm sure my angel arranged our meeting. More spoonfuls are received as each of our six children are born. A double dose of medicine from my 'Angel on my shoulder' came to me in the Blessed House.

My mother reappeared one day and visited us intermittently for several years in the Blessed House. Coffee, her cigarettes and quiet conversation as we sit around my dining table together are the tools that help my healing process. Sometimes we cook meals together in my sunny kitchen. Although I forgave her, the two or three hour visits every two years is not enough to mend the mother-daughter bond that was broken on that infamous day.

When my mother died at seventy-four years old I was obsessed with writing my story for my children. The urgency I feel drives me to write a book called The Red Dress, amidst raising five teenagers and one young adult, studying for my Masters Degree in Psychology, counseling clients and being a wife to my husband Tom.

The 'Angel on my shoulder' is my guide. I sit at my desk in the sitting area of our bedroom pouring my heart out for 132 pages. The spirits of the faithful parishioners before me meditating and praying in this very room help me write my story. When I finish and give the book to my six children I know my healing is complete. This cathartic experience frees my heart and soul from bondage.

My mother is in Heaven with the Lord and I know I've forgiven her. I am at peace!

I lost a mother but I gained another sister, Joann, from Ohio. The 'Angel on my shoulder' healed me in the Blessed House.

CHAPTER 9
A Celebration and a Calamity Coincide

There was no warning! We thought we had plenty of time.

The summer of our Silver Wedding Anniversary was lazy and hot. We were making plans for a trip to Washington, D.C. with the entire family. This was to be our last family trip together before the children left the nest. In the meantime we relished the pleasure of the sandy beach and cool Bay waters that adjoined our rolling front lawn. We enjoyed family time in our Blessed House. There were afternoons we swam vigorously followed by languishing contentedly in the warmth of the sun and sand reading a book. There were afternoons of intimate talks as we slowly walked on the shell filled beach followed by cocktails and hors 'de oeuvres while we watched in silent awe the sky become a brilliant artist palette of orange, red and gold colors as the sun set over the reflecting waters.

One Sunday in late August Tom and I were mysteriously presented with two tickets to an afternoon play at Trinity Square from our children. They whisked us off saying this was their Anniversary gift to us. Knowing how much we enjoy the theater, we accepted this lovely unexpected gift.

There was another momentous surprise awaiting us when we arrived home. What a feast our eyes beheld; a large elegant table laden with red lobsters, delicate white linens, polished silver, fine china, sparking crystal glasses and picturesque summer flowers on the sunlit windowed porch overlooking the rippling water. Amid the popping flash pictures Tom and I saw seated around the table our six children, brothers, a sister, sister-in-law, niece, nephew, mother and father. No wonder they sent us away to the theater. Our ecstacy was boundless because our family gave us the best present—themselves, working and playing together with us, so lovingly. Tom and I, satiated with food, family and love looked at each other and silently agreed that we made the right decision twenty-five years ago.

We were wallowing in these warm and wonderful feelings as the summer heated up during the last dog days of August and our plans were progressing for our trip. Vacations and schedules arranged and we were packing our suitcases when calamity struck.

There was no warning. Tom was given a severance pay and told he was no longer needed.

His fifteen years of loyal service came to an uncompromising abrupt end. My husband was on his own at forty-five years of age, with no job, no pension, no savings and no health or life insurance. I couldn't believe that this was happening to us again. Tom had worked very hard these past years and made an excellent salary that just covered our larger expenses. I pondered; What are we going to do now? Are we going to have to sell our beloved house that we have enjoyed for the past four years? Will our two children be able to continue in college? How will we send our other two children to college? I was enjoying my part-time counseling job more but making less money. We had an unwavering faith that God would see us through our tumult because our family prayed and worshiped together. We were strong and unified as a family and belonged to a church, the Genesis Community that would give us enormous support.

We could have cancelled our trip to Washington, D.C. but decided we needed this time together to celebrate being a family more than ever now. We received Blessings from Above in the form of two guardian angels. Bob and Jackie Markham, our old Buttonwoods friends offered to have our family as their guests at their home, just outside of Washington, D.C., in Vienna, VA; all eight of us. We were overcome by their generosity. We accepted their invitation. It was a wise decision. The Markhams were extraordinary hosts and we enjoyed their uplifting company. They enriched our journey immensely even cooking a special Anniversary dinner that was delicious and bountiful. We will forever be grateful to them. The joyous time strengthened us so that each member of the family cooperated and compromised. We helped each other get through the next very rough year. We relied on each others strength, encouragement and support during that terrible time of insecurity. We helped each other to face the realities of life that we cannot always control.

Hammers and Hopes

We thought we had plenty of time. Tom knew he would eventually strike out on his own someday. We did not expect it to be now. The family responded to the crisis. Tom began searching for a new job. "You're too old." or "you're overqualified." were the responses he received. Michael, who was a C.P.A. began searching for a business for sale. When he eventually found one, Tom, with much ingenuity, secured a loan with the backing of our Blessed home and became the owner of Cook Lead Hammer Co. We are now in business! Tom began his fresh new career in a cold dank dreary basement in East Providence surrounded by several pieces of immensely, shop-worn machinery, pallets of unmolten lead, a shabby desk and one chair. His predecessor instructed Tom and our son Steven, a team member, in the mechanics of firing the burner, melting the lead, pouring forms and gluing grips on handles that would ultimately result in finished lead hammers. He acquired a list of some existing mail order customers and learned shipping and mailing techniques. Now it was up to my husband who has a background in law school and Masters level in English, to turn this neglected flailing business into a profitable thriving venture that could support our large family and Blessed House. This was quite a challenge to Tom, but he felt he had no alternatives. He had not been able to find a job. God's grace continued to guide us!

We all pulled together. I increased my part time counseling to full-time. Michael helped with the accounting work and taxes. Steven brought his innovated and creative ideas to the shop and implemented them with hard work. Steven began as the chief lead hammer maker but it wasn't long before he revolutionized the business.

Relocating and Rebuilding

"Dad, we have to get out of this dreary basement," said Steve.

"I know. I'm looking at several rental properties but it'll be difficult and expensive to move all this heavy equipment."

"It'll be worth it, Dad. We can do it."

Steven commandeered the move to a new convenient, clean, well-lighted location close to home. They bought updated used machinery at an auction and Steven installed it as well as a more modern lead fire-burner. He mechanized the lead hammer process to save time, money and energy by designing and manufacturing new casting machinery. He initiated an advertising campaign including designing a brochure and selling on the road. He developed new hammers: bronze, copper and brass thus broadening the product line.

Tommy joined the workforce for one year as a hammer maker and shipping clerk. Dennis worked during the summertime taking over where he was needed in the shop or office. Tom kept the business humming, continuing his on-going precarious relationship with the banks; borrowing money for expansion; soliciting new customers and collecting from old ones and paying the bills. He also made sure the manufacturing was implemented and deadlines met, checked supplies and inventory, answered the telephone, taped name plates, secured UPS trucks, unloaded the lead as well as sweeping the floor and washing the bathroom. Eventually, our sons went off to college and the business grew so Tom was able to hire a full-time hammer maker.

He is a refugee from Cambodia whose influential family, who were loyal to the King, were massacred during Pol Pot's reign. He escaped by lying under dead bodies and pretending to be dead. Then, clad only in his shorts he walked for weeks, hiding and eating berries from trees, until he reached the safety of Thailand. After several years in the Thailand Refugee Camp he came to R.I. to live a free life. He continues to be a loyal, industrious chief hammer maker at our family business. We have so much to be thankful for; family, friends, a home, a business and freedom!

CHAPTER 10
Heaven's On My Beach

"Heaven's not behind the clouds,
It's for us to find it here."

I am listening to the haunting warm vocals and acoustic guitar of Pat Surface singing these provocative words from Belleau Wood as I sit by the sea. He is accompanied by the cello, violin and subtle percussion and this music permeates my heart and soul. I have found my Heaven. It is the peace and love I feel when I am at the sea. Music By The Sea!

Living on the beach on Greenwich Bay brings me many pleasures. I have always loved to swim. Every summer day at high-tide is my special swim-time. I walk out the front door and swim in the warm Bay waters. The sensuous feel of the water all over my body and my rhythmic strokes transport me into nirvana. I am surprised when my twenty, sometimes thirty minute routine comes to an end. I lose all track of time. Not wanting to leave the soothing waters I play with the gentle waves until I tire. My friends call me 'Esther Williams'. Swimming In The Sea!

Another delight is walking along the seashore breathing in the bracing air as I take my brisk early morning exercise. My bare feet sink into the soft warm sand and my mind soars thanking a generous God for His gifts of Nature's beauty; beauty in the brilliant sun in a clear blue sky; beauty in the beach sand dotted with opened seashells; beauty in the cooling rippling waters. Walking By The Sea!

My passion for reading and sometimes writing is enhanced when I sit on my beach under an umbrella or in the shade of our swamp maple tree above the sea waters, discovering new relationships, unfolding mysteries and enlightenment. Reading By The Sea!

Just to sit and gaze at the sea is so soothing, so uplifting. May through September we have a front row seat on our deck or beach for the sailboat races and regattas on Greenwich Bay. This is a spectacle of free entertainment. Looking to our right we can see a Yacht Club and three Marinas nestled into the coves. Each Marina has a race one night a week. The neon orange markers are in place, the starting gun explodes and the race is on, within our view. The parade of white-sailed boats gracefully gliding and tacking (turning) around the orange markers is becoming and becalming. The twenty-five or thirty foot boats follow one another in a line so closely they merge together as one. The sound of the sails tacking and filling up with wind or sometimes ruffling is very pleasant. The East Greenwich Yacht Club Sail covers more distance. Some evenings we have dinner at our picnic table on the deck and watch the boats sail past our ideal viewing stand and become a speck on the horizon. An hour later as we're finishing dinner they return tacking back and forth with the wind. If the wind has slowed significantly they unfurl their giant colorful spinnaker sails in front of their mainsail. Ths spectacular sight is breathtaking. Each sail is a melange of bright colors; green, yellow, orange, red, blues and has a different pattern indigenous to their particular sailboat. Sipping a glass of wine or beer we watch the latecomers race the darkness into port.

In the daytime schools of small white sail J boats dot the Bay with the student-children at the helm. No matter what time of day there is a flurry of activity as many boats sail or motor past our home to other ports, seaside restaurants, seaside nightclubs and other sea towns—Jamestown, Wickford, Newport. Beyond Newport they sail into the open ocean. Many boats continue to Block Island, a popular boating island several miles off the coast of R.I. In our Blessed House surrounded by windows on three sides, I thank the Lord that I can enjoy this view inside or outside, rain or shine or hurricane. Gazing At The Sea! I am whole.

I see, feel, hear, taste and smell the Sea's pleasures.

I can't think of anywhere else I would feel this mystical peace and contentment. I have found my...

Heaven On My Beach
Music By The Sea
Swimming By The Sea
Walking By the Sea
Reading By the Sea
Gazing At The Sea

CHAPTER 11
Sisters and 27 Cousins

The rented van trudged up the mountain winding around past the olive trees, the grape arbors, the donkeys and the goats to the hill town of Savoia di Lucania. My Uncle Frank, his wife Rita and several cousins were searching for our Italian family's roots. Irma approached a wrinkled, white-haired lady in a long back dress sitting on a bench in the square.

"Go away, go away," she gestured and shrieked in Italian as she ran away before my cousin could even speak. Then a younger woman appeared in the doorway.

"Do you speak English?" Uncle Frank inquired.

"Una Momento, Una Momento," she called out as she dashed through the alley to summon her husband. In a few minutes a muscular bearded man with big brown eyes and aquiline nose arrived. He is the only person in the village who spoke English. Introductions were made.

"My parents were born in this village. We're visiting from the U.S. and would like to look around and maybe get a copy of their birth or marriage certificate."

"What's the name and where in the U.S. are you from?" asked Archi, the village physician, in perfect English but with a Brooklyn accent. He gave the guests a tour of the village, the old homestead and the Church. Communications began. He also procured a document, Rocco and Angelina Agoglia's marriage certificate at St. Rocco's Church, my grandparents.

I heard the story about how my grandmother walked down that steep mountain from her village with a baby in her arms and two young children at her side and continued walking several more miles to the nearest train station. After a train ride to the harbour they boarded a ship to take them to America. She eventually joined her husband who preceded her and was working on a railroad in the U.S. How desperate their lives must have been at that time to leave their small village and cross an ocean for a better life in America.

Angelina and Rocco came to live in R.I. The family grew to seven sons and three daughters. When the children were in school, I am told, a teacher suggested that the Agoglia name was too unwieldy should sons go into business. She suggested a name change. She picked Olean from the map, Olean, N.Y., where no one had ever been. Her premonition came true: six sons opened their own businesses. My grandfather settled into farming and wine making, instilling a strong work ethic in his children.

Several years later, my sister Beverly, six cousins and I climb the same mountain in a nine passenger dented van to visit the village of our grandparents, Rocco and Angelina (Agoglia) Olean.

When cousins Lillian, Arlene, Joe, Irma, Paul, his wife Sharon, Beverly and I climb out of the van into the square many villagers come to view the spectacle. They do not run away. They are silent but the schoolboys call out,

"Hey Americano! Hallo Americano!" Another voice from the third floor window of the brick school shouts,

"I'm Giovanni! Hallo Cowboy!" Both boys duck inside. Cousin Joe, who drove the van, is conspicuous in his large white cowboy hat, denim jeans and black boots.

We are embraced by Archi and his family and treated like royalty. Discoveries are made. Archi, a physician, was born in the U.S. and received medical training and degrees in Italy. His parents emigrated to Brooklyn, N.Y. before he was born but continued to vacation in Savoia for many years. They married and live in the village with their two sons, Alberto and Rocco. Archi is also an agronomist, studying and interpreting water and soil needs for Europe for the Italian government.

"Archi, can you show us where our grandparents lived?" we ask.

He gives us a tour of the ancient village. Leaving the square we walk upward along a maze of narrow passageways passing for streets. Imagine my surprise when I see a donkey carrying groceries up the car-free alley to an upper level. As I look at the houses all connected and layered on top of each other I am reminded of a stack of rectangular pancakes. A boarded up castle battered by an earthquake is at the summit towering over the houses. After a few turns I am lost in this labyrinth of alleys when No. 10 Selfino appears.

"This is the house your grandparents lived in," says Archi. Large purple flowers blooming in a black wrought iron flower box on the balcony dress up the plain facade of No. 10. The balcony opens up before me revealing a green expanse of valleys which is both soothing and exhilarating.

"What's that big opening below their balcony?" Lillian inquires.

"That's where you grandparents housed their animals. Most people had donkeys and goats, some still have them."

"So we noticed," exclaimed Arlene.

When we reached the square we see a man driving a tractor and pulling a large red wagon with a woman sitting among the piles of grapes. I feel like I am stepping back and forth in time.

"That couple is returning from picking their grapes on the other side of the mountain. Most villagers grow grapes, press them and bottle their own wine. Some grow olives and make olive oil. This is what they've done for many generations," said Archi.

"Do they sell their wine and olive oil?" asked Sharon.

"Oh, yes. I'll take you to our little store in the village later."

"We'd love to take some home," we all chime in.

The smell of freshly baked bread drifts through the door as we enter another cousin's bakery. We meet Marlena and Maria whose father owns the bakery. They are studying English in college and are anxious to practice the language with us. We sample warm pepper biscuits and listen to halting English from these delightful younger cousins, whetting our appetite for more of both.

The next stop on the tour is Archi and Carmella's house where we are invited to dine. Carmella and her mother Philomena have been cooking all day. The smell of garlic and tomato gravy lure us into their compact home. The house has three levels and more apartments on top of it. We are not aware of the tight quarters we are in as we all sit around a large table because the family bonds are warm and simmering just like the gravy pot on the stove. They ask about our families and what our life is like in the U.S.A. Archi interprets for us. We listen to Rocco read English from his first grade reader. We talk and eat. Just like Grandmother Angelina's kitchen, we are served an abundance of love and savory food all afternoon; pasta with fresh-picked mushrooms, stuffed eggplant, sausage and peppers, friend chicken, Italian crusty bread, cauliflower and carrot salad, chocolate cake and homemade red wine. When we are so full we can't eat anymore, espresso coffee and peach vodka and lemoncello is served in frozen glasses.

Archi has arranged for us to stay at the Hotel Beauganville, a 5 star hotel a few miles from the village. My sister Beverly and I are sharing a room in this newly-opened, reasonably-priced hotel. The sweeping views of flowering mountains, lush valleys and more mountain top villages merging with the sky gives us a feeling of reverence.

The sweet smelling mountain air energizes and calms us. My senses are reeling with intoxicating new sights, sounds, smells, tastes and touches but the ultimate feast for my heart is the love that is brewing between my sister and me.

Because we were separated at our young ages of four and eight years we did not have a close sisterly relationship. We were sent to a Catholic boarding school when my mother abandoned the family. We lived in different buildings. After a few months my sister was sent to live with a succession of relatives while I remained at boarding school. We saw each other infrequently, sometimes on holidays or summer days. When my father remarried several years later, my sister, younger brother Richard and I were force-fed into a family. I wasn't always a good big sister but Beverly was always there for me.

Our relationship began to improve years later when I was married and had six children. Auntie Beverly is a Super Aunt, Babysitter and Friend to her two nieces and four nephews. She even rescued my family one snowy December day before Christmas. Auctioneers startled us as they planted red flags on our lawn and were about to sell our ranch house. We were behind in our mortgage payments because my husband recently closed his flailing fence business. We thought arrangements with the bank had been made. I called my sister at work.

"Beverly, the lawyer is going to auction off our house if we don't come up with five hundred dollars in thirty minutes," I cried in despair.

"I'll be right there as soon as I can get the money out of my savings account at the bank," she replied without hesitation.

She careened through the eighteen miles of roads so we could give the money to the imperturbital lawyer and not be homeless. I remember that with love and gratitude.

Since Tom and I moved into the Blessed House my sister is a frequent visitor. On holidays, birthdays and special occasions we invite grandparents, aunts, uncles, cousins and sometimes friends to share a home-cooked meal. I enjoy the cooking and the spirited boisterousness that comes with family gatherings. As sisters, Beverly and I can be hot or cold, marinating or boiling over.

In Savoia di Laconia there is a freshness in our kinship and it extends beyond Beverly and I to our six American cousins. Every evening we meet in the larger room in our hotel. Arlene and Lillian, who are also sisters, share this room with Irma. Irma's brother Joe has a room across the hall and so do her brother Paul and his wife Sharon. We chatter and laugh loudly like old friends in between mouthfuls of cheese, dry sausage and crackers and wine and Sambuca.

"I can't believe that we went to Mass at St. Rocco's Church, in the village, the same church our grandparents were married in over one hundred years ago," said Irma.

"When we opened those plain wooden doors I was astonished by the brightness and beauty inside," added Paul.

"Wasn't it gorgeous the way the light from those tall windows lit up all the marble?" said Lillian.

"I've never seen so many different colors of marble. It was everywhere, the columns, the floor, even the walls," said Arlene.

"Did you see those tapestries on the wall?" asked Lillian. "Maria said they were done by a famous artist in the 18th Century."

"I was wondering how a Church built in the 16th Century could survive in this poor village. The earthquake didn't even touch it," I added.

"I couldn't concentrate on the Mass with Rocco and Alberto giggling on the altar," said Irma.

"Didn't they look cute in their red and white altar-boy cassocks?" said Sharon.

"They even stood up and posed for you when you took out your camera," said Joe.

"I love meeting all our new cousins, especially after Mass when all the town folk gather in the square talking and 'looking over' the Americans. They made us feel so welcomed." said Beverly.

After Mass we are invited to Philomena's house where they have prepared a 'light lunch'. We are bombarded by a potpourri of Smells and Tastes; fried peppers, sausages, provolone, etc. Sounds; animated loud conversations in Italian and English, laughter and Sights; sitting at a large table that is placed wall to wall in the crowded living room, relatives of all ages coming and going, eating and talking. It was an Italian Circus or a Celebratory Feast!

Marlena and Maria, our young cousins from the village, spend many hours searching the ancient documents in Savoia's town hall for the Agoglia/Martone ancestors. Visitors are not allowed to see or touch these fragile records.

Back at Archi's house, his young sons serve us appetizers as we watch Archi, Maria and Marlena put this recent information on the computer.

When they assemble a complete family tree we are handed a gift that is a connection to our family's roots.

Our last evening we decide to take all our cousins, however many there are, who live in the village, out to dinner. Imagine our surprise when twenty-seven relatives join us at La Bruchetta, the only restaurant in Savoia.

Another cousin, the restaurant owner, sets up a very long table for us. Several courses of family style food: ham, prosciuto, salami, fresh mozzarella, eggplant, fried and roasted peppers and zucchini is the first course of Antipasto. Dishes are refilled frequently. The second course is the specialty of the house—thin pizzas, platters of vegetable pizza, four cheese pizza, bruschetta pizza, and tomato-cheese pizza quickly empty and are refilled. The third course is french fries?? We're not such Italian chauvinists that we refuse them. Bottles of wine and beer are never-ending.

In between bites of food, communication in two languages plus animated gestures and laughter is loud. We have three interpreters. This is one of those times when we Americans wish we had learned the Italian language from our parents. Happy Birthday is sung to five cousins celebrating a birthday that week and we share their large cake for dessert. Carmella's father Rocco plays the accordion and several cousins, American and Italian, dance and sing together. The evening ended with the entire family in a group picture and a nominal bill for the American cousins.

We felt like family in Savoia di Laconia from the moment we stepped onto its soil. Meeting our kind-hearted, friendly relatives is an exceptional blessing. We will remember these special moments, together as family, long after we find our way home. We shared our happiness eating at their tables, praying in St. Rocco's Church, watching them research our family tree, having them as our personal guides on sightseeing trips and communicating, sometimes without words.

Our adventure did not end in the village. We tried to check out of the hotel at 5:00 a.m. because we were to continue our long journey to Rome. The night clerk, who spoke only Italian, could not check us out. After many futile attempts to communicate with him we left our credit card numbers on his desk for future check-out. The clerk was baffled. He did not want us to leave. Nonetheless, we all piled into the van and Joe drove for five hours.

Arriving at the Alfi Hotel in the heart of Rome we are told at the desk that we were going to be arrested because we didn't pay our bill. Several phone calls are exchanged, in Italian and English. Finally we enlist Archi, by phone. His intervention resolves the dispute. Now, we are allowed to check in to this hotel.

"Where have you been?" Beverly screamed at me as I lay sprawled on our hotel bed after a day of sightseeing in Rome.

"We've been searching all over the streets for you. We went into every shop. What are you doing here? I told you not to leave my side. Look at you...lying on the bed as if nothing happened. You caused me so much aggravation!"

When my sister came up for a breath of air I tried to explain that when I looked around she and Joe weren't there.

"After looking in the shops I decided the best thing for me to do was to walk home." I said.

"Your sister was really worried about you. I suggested we return to the hotel. She didn't think you even knew the way here," said cousin Joe.

"All I kept thinking about was how was I going to tell my brother-in-law that I lost his wife in Rome. And here you are resting in the hotel.

Don't you ever do that to me again." Beverly admonished.

I stifled a laugh and thought. After that tirade if I wasn't convinced that my little sister really cares about her big sister, I do now!

Later, sitting on the hotel balcony overlooking the flowered courtyard, Beverly, Joe and I smoothed down our worries with ruby-red Chianti wine, crisp crackers and provolone cheese. They bought this wine in the liquor store, where I had never looked.

When we returned home I invited Beverly to a meatball and spaghetti dinner at the Blessed House. We reminisced about our excursions in Southern Italy: watching dripping Stalagmites in an ancient cave; walking on the rocks of a circular archeological site; observing a wedding couple taking pictures at a 13th century Monastery that was taken over by the German's for P.O.W.'s during W.W. II, climbing around the abandoned Sassi Cave houses, driving the narrow cliff road of the Amalfi drive, lunching in the seaside town of Positano while the nude sunbathers roam the beach below, and buying art treasures in the quaint town of Sorrento.

"Remember how you tried to tame my frizzy curls with your special conditioner?" asked Beverly.

"Oh, yes, and how about you trying to curl my eyelashes with a curler?" I added.

"Neither of us was successful, but it was fun trying."

We are simmering as sisters now. We try to prolong these good feelings. We agreed that touring Southern Italy and Rome, listening to Pope John's inspirational sermon in many languages, examining the crypts in a sub-basement under St. Peter's Basilica (a special tour because cousin Paul's company Bose installed the Cathedral's sound system) were magnificent but did not compare to being in Savoia di Laconia, our grandparents birthplace, meeting our 27 cousins and enjoying our

American cousins. Our fires are lit, now we need to keep them glowing. The spirit of the Blessed House is alive on two continents. The blessings stretch across the ocean to our relatives in the Village of Savoia di Laconia. Our cousins brought my sister Beverly and me together on this trip.

Beverly and I brainstorm ideas.

"Why don't we correspond by e-mail to our relatives in Savoia?"

"Why don't we have a party in this house?"

"Why don't we invite our American cousins?"

"Why don't we cook together in the Blessed House?"

"Why don't we revive our Italian Family Reunion tradition?"

"Why don't we call it our Italian First-Cousins Reunion?"

The house speaks.

"This is a house of love and bounty

Like the spirits of those who lived

before you, throw wide the door

and give love and sustenance to

all who come here."

For many years while my children were growing up, the Olean clan of two hundred gathered at Uncle Tom's farm. It was a wonderful way to stay connected to family and have a good time. Uncle Tom has since died and so have his nine siblings and all but two elderly spouses. The Reunion tradition died out for many years. We decided to have a First-Cousins Reunion, all thirty-five will be invited plus spouses, no children.

Beverly and I devoted many hours planning, talking and sending invitations together. We did all the cooking together in the Blessed House. The intimacy between us is in the pot on the stove and we stir and season it frequently. We cooked two large lasagnas. I mixed the meats and sauce as she mixed the three cheeses. We anticipated each others needs, combining our efforts and having fun. I raked the clams and Beverly washed and chopped them. Then we cooked and filled the shells for Stuffed Quahogs/Stuffies. We cooked spinach pies. She cooked the spinach and I rolled the dough. We assembled the pies with black olives, garlic and extra virgin olive oil together. We baked a cheesecake and pies: blueberry and apple. We put them in the oven while we washed the utensils, dishes and pans. When the cooking was done we decorated the house, the porch and the front lawn. Four long tables and chairs sit on the lawn surrounded by the periwinkle blue flowering weeds. Two round tables are on the deck with umbrellas overhead. The blue-green waters reflect the sunshine which is skimming along with the gentle waves.

Cousins arrive from R.I., Connecticut and New York. We all move around with ease making sure we talk to all our cousins. We share the latest weddings, divorces, grandchildren, aches, pains and surgeries and some retirements. The home-cooked food is served and eaten in stages all afternoon. When the sun begins to set over the water we assemble on the lawn while my son takes our picture. Everyone enjoyed themselves so much, our kindness and generosity is spread to our cousins from Westerly. We are invited next year to another Cousins Reunion.

We have a new tradition. Beverly and I are now soul-sisters. We continue to bake, Manga and party together often. We're cookin now with joy in our hearts.

Deep down I always knew that you can never give up on family. They can enrich your life and it's worth the effort.

Barbara's Lasagna Recipe
Homemade Spaghetti Sauce—Red Gravy

1 lb. Italian sausage, ½ sweet, ½ hot

½ stick pepperoni sausage

1 lb. ground beef

32 oz. carton full fat Ricotta cheese

1 lb. Mozzarella cheese, shredded

½ cup grated Parmesan cheese

1/4 cup chopped fresh parsley

2 eggs, slightly beaten

Dash ground black pepper

1 & 1/4 lb. lasagna pasta

Saute the ground beef and drain grease.

Chop cooked sausage in food processor.

Mix ground beef, sausage and some red gravy together in a bowl.

Blend Ricotta cheese, shredded Mozzarella cheese and Parmesan cheese together.

Mix the 2 eggs, parsley and pepper into the cheese mixture.

Leave in bowl.

Boil the lasagna pasta for 5 minutes and drain.

Cover the bottom of a large lasagna pan or casserole with red gravy.

Place one layer of pasta in the dish overlapping the pieces.

Spoon the ground beef/sausage/gravy mixture on top of the pasta.

Then spoon the cheese mixture on top of the meat mixture.

Continue the layers until all ingredients are used.

Cover with sauce, sprinkle Parmesan cheese and add thin slices of Mozzarella cheese for garnish.

Bake at 350 degrees for 40-50 minutes or until bubbly.
Let stand 10 minutes before serving.
Serve in squares.

Manga ! Manga !

CHAPTER 12
Letters from the Bible and the Bedroom

Paul's Letter to the Phillipians Chapter 4-Verse 4, New Testament
Joy and Peace

"Rejoice in the Lord always. I shall say it again: rejoice. Your kindness should be known to all. The Lord is near. Have no anxiety at all, but in everything, by prayer and petition, with thanksgiving, make your requests known to God. Then the peace of God that surpasses all understanding will guard your hearts and minds in Christ Jesus."

Nov. 27, 1986

Dear Bill,

I am so sorry to hear about your recent open heart surgery. I'm sure you had excellent doctors and good nursing care. Alice will take good care of you now that you are home.

I am sitting in bed at home writing to you recovering from recent major gall bladder surgery. Healing at home with family around eases the pain of surgery. I feel such peace in my heart in these wonderful surroundings.

I want to tell you about my hospital spiritual visit. For my first twenty-four hours post surgery I was in a stupor of pain and narcotics. The next morning I woke early before the hospital sounds awakened and had an awesome uplifting experience. My eyes were drawn to a shaft of light coming through a crack under the window shade. As it became brighter and brighter it lit up the room. I was entranced. It paralyzed me. I immediately felt someone holding my right hand. The touch was warm and welcoming. It traveled throughout my whole body showering me with overwhelming joy and peace. In the silence of the room I heard these words in my heart and soul and body

"Get up and walk, go home."

I felt the Lord holding my hand and telling me that I was going to heal. The peaceful painless feeling lasted about a minute and was replaced with an urgency to leave the hospital.

When the nurse arrived I said, "Please disconnect all my tubes. I am going to eat breakfast and walk to the bathroom so I can go home tomorrow."

"Oh, no, it's much too soon after surgery. The doctor will not allow it. You haven't even been out of bed yet," she answered.

"Watch me, I can do it," I said and I did. I had the Lord's hand guiding me as I groped my way down the hall to the nurses desk to show her. I ate my meals, walked to the bathroom and drank fluids while taking milder pain pills. The next morning when the doctor arrived at 10:00 A.M. I announced, "I am going home today. It's my birthday tomorrow and I want to eat cake and ice cream with my family. The best place for me to heal is in my peaceful bedroom at home overlooking the Bay waters."

"Well, it's a bit unusual. Normally we keep gall bladder patients in for five days," looking at my chart, "I see you have been doing everything you are supposed to. Is there anyone at home to take care of you?"

"Yes, my husband will be there." Two hours later when my visitors arrived at the hospital I was at home. I celebrated my birthday surrounded by my family. I feel God's blessing all around me.

I believe the Lord touched me for a reason. I am reaching out to you to tell you that God loves you. Pray and ask Him to heal you. Read The New Testament Chpt 4, Verse 4. This passage was helpful to me. You have my love and prayers for a speedy recovery.

Love, Barbara

Nov. 27, 1986

Dear Tom,

I am so sorry to hear about your recent hip surgery and replacement due to cancer. It must be very difficult for you to be in a body cast. I'm sure Donna will take good care of you now that you are home. It's great that she's a nurse.

I am sitting in bed...I repeated as above.

Dear Barbara,

I did not have hip surgery. I had open heart surgery. My name is not Bill. I think this letter belongs to someone else. I thought it was interesting.

Love, Tom

Dear Barbara,

I had hip surgery not open-heart surgery. My name is Bill. I think this letter belongs to someone else.

Love, Bill

Several years later I wrote a letter of encouragement and prayers to my friend Maryann who had a thyroid operation for cancer. She mailed back to me my empty open unsealed envelope that was addressed to her.

Dear Barbara,

What was it you wanted to say? Maryann. This was scrawled across the envelope.

Dear Lord,

I felt your guiding hand when I reached out to my friends. If you want me to continue to work for You, I NEED HELP!

Love, Barbara

P.S. Thanks for my healing and my friends.

CHAPTER 13
Getting Saved

"What are you doing in my house? Get away from here or I'll call the cops," I yelled at the intruder with the choir boy face as he exited the back screen door on the lower level of my house. He tried to speak, mumbled some words but I quickly shut him up.

"Get out and don't you ever show up here again," I continued screaming from my perch up on the deck stairway. He quickly ran away with his Michael Jordan sneakers on his feet and his bulging gray backpack on his back. I was not frightened, just angry, as I immediately went back inside the house to call my husband.

"Cook Hammer Co," answered my practical son, Steven.

"Is Dad there? I need to talk to him right now."

"No, he's out at the bank. What's the matter Mom?"

"You tell Dad that he'd better bring home a new lock for the back door or don't come home."

"What happened?"

"I was just walking out the upstairs door when I saw an intruder coming out of the recreation room door. I told Dad a million times to get a new lock for that door. It's impossible to see or hear anyone from in the house.

"Are you okay, Mom?"

"Yes, I chased him away."

"Alright, Mom, I'll tell Dad when he comes in."

With my anger at my husband spent I continued on my original journey to the grocery store.

When I arrived home I came to an abrupt stop. Four white and black police cars with blue flashing lights were blocking my street, my driveway and my house. A police officer approached me.

"Who are you and what is your business here."

"I live here. I'm Barbara Malone."

"Please step out of the car, Ma'am."

"What's going on? Why are you here? What happened?, the anxiety reflecting in my voice.

"Just answer the questions. Where were you?"

"I've been grocery shopping. Why?"

The officer continued, "Do you recognize this backpack, Mam?"

"Yes, a man was coming out of my back screen door and he had it on his back. Why?"

"We received a call about an intruder at this address, possible abduction. We have been searching the neighborhood for both of you. We found the intruder, interrogated him and let him go. If he ever comes back into this neighborhood he will be arrested," he reported. Confusing thoughts were swirling around in my head when I looked up and saw my son Dennis standing in the doorway. He was supposed to be working at the Hammer Co.

"Mom, Steven told me what happened so I called you back and there was no answer. I was worried so I called the police. Are you alright?"

The day the cops surrounded my house; my sensitive son was trying to save me, the intruder with the choir boy face was trying to save my soul, and my procrastinating husband was trying to save himself from another endless chore.

I was naked and you clothed me.

Chapter 14
In My Home Office

The Roller Skating Queen

"Barbara, she shouted," you saved my life! What are you doing here?"

This was my greeting as I walked into the emergency room of our local hospital to begin volunteering. I was immediately enveloped into a strong endearing hug as she repeated, "You saved my life!"

My mind flipped through the index in my brain trying to discover who was hugging me. Whose life did I save? I just arrived. After a jolt to my memory I recognized Jean, the Roller Skating Queen.

My home office in this Blessed house was a haven for abused women, grieving widows, widowers and children, depressed, anxious clients and troubled marital partners, anyone who was in pain. When I became a psychotherapist I had many years previous experience as a nurse taking care of patients physical needs. My approach to psychotherapy is holistic. I address clients diet, exercise, recreation, care of their soul as well as their emotional needs. In this book-lined room with comfortable chairs and couch I feel a strong connection to Father St. Jean. This humble priest, that I never knew, was a healer of people, body and soul. My clients tell me they want what I have—peace and joy. I am blessed by the Lord and continue to heal people body and soul in this tranquil room where this priest died.

"Oh, I'm so glad to see you, Barbara. I have thought of you often and how you helped me change my life," Jean gushed.

This emergency room nurse was one of my clients twenty years ago.

"I hate myself. I'm so fat and ugly. I have no energy. I'm tired all the time. I'm so unhappy. Can you help me?" Jean asked on our first visit.

She was a young married nurse with three children, depressed, overweight with low self-esteem. The first piece of the puzzle. Subsequent weeks revealed more pieces of the puzzle. When completed the picture showed Jean was married to, you guessed it, the Roller Skating King. They met at the Providence Roller Skating Rink and were crowned the King and Queen. They rolled around the rinks displaying their expert techniques for the crowds. They were young, talented and riding high! The King wanted control and perfectionism in their marriage. He wanted his Queen to be slim and perfect forever. When Jean finished therapy she gained back her confidence and began to love and believe in herself.

"Thanks for helping me realize I was in a no-win emotionally abusive relationship. Nothing I ever did was good enough for him. Everything was my fault he said and I believed him. I finally left him, lost weight, gained more nursing degrees and am happy. He quickly married a slim aerobics instructor but it didn't last. I'm a head nurse in this emergency room now. I've had many articles published in professional nursing magazines. I love my work and my children are great. Thank you so much," said Jean, as she caught me up on the last twenty years. Then she took me around and introduced me to the staff.

"This is my therapist. She saved my life."

Before each session I pray to God for guidance to relieve my clients pain and help them be at peace. I am grateful for His blessings that channeled through me to the Roller Skating Queen.

Esmeralda, The Psychic

I was not as successful with Regina, the Dentist's wife.

"Can you help my marriage? I don't want to leave my husband. We've been married for twenty years and have four daughters," said the elegantly dressed genteel woman. The pieces of the puzzle began to unscramble as she revealed in subsequent visits that she had many hospital visits. Her most recent one they recommended counseling again, after she suffered a broken jaw, loss of teeth, a black eye and several body bruises from the Dentist.

"I don't want to leave my husband. I dread being a divorced single woman. I'm used to a certain lifestyle and I'm convinced he's squirreling away our money so I can't get at it," she cried.

During the many sessions of psychotherapy I said, "The bottom line is that your life is in danger."

"Oh, no," she emphasized. "He won't hit me again. He promised. He's so sorry. He bought me this beautiful diamond bracelet."

Regina ultimately left therapy and I did not hear from her until a year later she called. "Barbara, I have to tell you that I finally left my husband. I thought you would like to know. I called up that telephone psychic, Esmeralda one day. You know, the one you see the numbers on your television screen?"

"Yes, I have seen her ads," I answered.

"Well, she told me that if I didn't leave my husband I'll be dead in two months. Isn't that great! She knew all about me and for thirty-five dollars she helped me."

That evening I related this story to my husband. We shared a laugh as he said, "Well, counselor, you've now been replaced by a telephone psychic."

"What next," I sighed.

The Lord works in mysterious ways!

Guiding Pilgrims to Paradise

"Will you pray with me before we begin?" asked my first client at the St. Vincent de Paul family health center. I hesitated. I was thrown off-guard. No one ever asked me to pray with them in my counseling sessions in my office in the Blessed House. My mind raced. Is this professional? Can I do this and still be respected as a psychiatric nurse therapist? What prayers will I say? I looked into this forlorn woman's sad eyes and knew what I had to do. I grasped her hands in mine and began,

"Dear Lord please help Jenna to be filled with Your love and find peace in her heart," the Holy Spirit flowed from my lips.

"Amen," she continued. "My only daughter was murdered two years ago. I am still hurting. They haven't found the man who killed her."

The next client was Louise, a sixteen year old young woman who was raped and couldn't tell anyone fearing her mother would throw her out of the house.

I continued praying and listening to these disadvantaged women throughout the morning. They were suffering but had a strong faith in the Lord and hopes for a better life.

I had my doubts about reaching this indigent population. In my private practice I see middle-class suburban insured clients. They are husbands and wives with relationship problems; families with teenagers having communication problems, women burdened with the guilt of a past abortion and widows, widowers and children overwhelmed by their sudden losses. I was very content counseling at home and teaching part-time at a local college. How did I get into this situation? Was it a coincidence or did the Lord lead me here for a reason?

One evening my husband and I finally agreed to accompany my youngest son, Dennis, to a prayer meeting that he had been attending for several months. He was anxious to share his renewed relationship with Christ. After the meeting he introduced us to several people. Then, he took me by the hand,

"Mom, I want to introduce you to Dr. Mello. Dr. Mello, my mother, Barbara Malone."

"Dr. Mello!" I exclaimed.

"This is your mom, Dennis, Barbara Malone, the therapist that I have been dying to meet?" he questioned. I smiled yes and he immediately embraced me in a watertight hug. We both spoke at the same time.

"I had no idea you were Dennis' mother. He's such a great kid."

"I'm so glad we finally get to meet each other. Thank you so much for all the clients you have referred to me."

"Thank you for helping me out. You did a wonderful job. The patients reported back to me."

Dr. Mello had been referring his patients to me from his upscale private medical practice in wealthy East Greenwich, for several years. Many came to him with various physical symptoms like backaches, headaches, stomach upsets and malaise that had no basis in physical disease. He took a chance with me because of my nursing background and referred patients for a holistic therapeutic approach—emotional, physical and spiritual, although we had never spoken.

"Mom, Dr. Mello is the doctor at the St. Vincent's family center now," clarified Dennis. Dr. Mello responded "I'm so glad that we met tonight because we desperately need a volunteer therapist. Can you spare a few hours a week?"

"Of course I can," I replied without hesitation. I felt in my heart that this was where I should be even though I had a very busy schedule. Dr. Mello gave up his lucrative practice and lives and works among the poor for a paltry sum. I knew it would be a privilege to work with this saintly doctor and be a member of his team.

As I began each volunteer counseling session praying with my clients, the Holy Spirit continued to flow into my being, dissolving my doubts and guiding my words. This experience changed my professional approach with my private clients in our Blessed House office. I find it easier to speak about God and salvation. I don't hesitate to teach clients how to prayerfully meditate. I pass out Rosary Beads and instructions to those who are interested. I am amazed that so many clients are seeking spiritual as well as emotional healing. I bond with clients quicker and in a special way. Many times I don't know what I am going to say to clients but I feel the Lord in my heart, my mind and my being as He speaks through me during our fifty minute sessions. I am trying to lighten and guide these pilgrims path so they will find their way to Paradise.

CHAPTER 15
Our Seminarian and Our Scholar

Home for Healing

"Mom, can I move back home? I'm having financial problems and I'm all mixed up and don't feel well. I dropped out of school," came his anguished plea.

What do you do when your adult son returns home after a disconcerted shock from childhood emerges and screeches his unfolding life to a halt?

Our Scholar was excelling in an accelerated M.B.A. program in college. He thrived on academic activities and was totally committed to the program. Building pressures from a childhood trauma, impending bankruptcy, and a newly diagnosed chronic disease, forced him to take an incomplete on his two last subjects. Our whole family was affected.

What do you do? You hold your shattered heart together and be strong. You accept him into his former home, giving him a safe, comfortable, private room and lots of love. You pray, meditate and listen to his anguished voice. You seek professional help. You provide nourishing meals and caring comfort in the night. You accept that sometimes he may not be able to be with family and friends. You accept that your Scholar, on the last minute, may have to stay in his room and cannot enjoy his younger brother's wedding festivities at our house even though he ordered a tux to be an usher. You accept that some nights he cannot be left alone with his terrors. You give him time to heal.

"Mom, I need to come home from Ontario. I've left the priesthood and want to rethink my career."

One year ago, fifty of our family and friends were seated on chairs and blankets on our front lawn celebrating a Mass for our future Seminarian. We were praying for our youngest son who was leaving for the priesthood in Canada. We draped linens over a portable bar for an altar facing the Bay waters. The salt-filled air breathed around us as we sang hymns of praise to Our Lord. I wondered if Father St. Jean, before us, ever said any outdoor Masses in this peaceful setting surrounded by God's natural beauty. During his homily, our priest compared this vista to his recent visit to the Sea of Galilee in Jerusalem where Jesus spoke to the multitudes. Our hearts were bursting with love, prayers and good wishes for our future Seminarian. We did not see him for one year while he devoted himself to his studies.

We gave our former Seminarian a private bedroom, healthy meals and lots of love and time to readjust and contemplate his future.

You pray to Father St. Jean and others before us that the healing powers in this Blessed House will come to our family.

When the winter of suffering lightens you give the Scholar projects to

keep him busy. He began by building a twenty foot ramp so we would have easy access to the beach.

A forty foot deck along the front of our house was deteriorating. We provided the materials for our Seminarian and Scholar to replace the deck. They designed and built a new wrap-around deck doubling the space. Carpentry was a new skill our sons developed on their own. That summer healing was taking place, the old rotted deck was demolished along with the rotted sill beams that were the foundation on the front of the old house. In it's place, peace seeped into their hearts as they jacked up the front of the house, replaced the foundation, built a larger deck with weather-resistant lumber and strenuously labored for many hours. Another son, who lived at home, joined the work force when he came home from work. So did our two and one-half year old grandson, Bobby, who banged nails beside them, lightening our mood immensely. When September came the deck was finished but they were not ready for the world yet, so we provided them with shingles for our oversized garage.

You rejoice and thank God for His blessings! He sent His blessings and healing to our sons and family in our Blessed House. I could feel the spirits who lived here before us melting away our Scholar's pain. His demons are gone. His disease is under control with medication. Today, our Scholar and Seminarian are on a different flourishing path, taking over the family business so that Tom and I can winter in Florida. I thank the Lord every day.

Our Blessed House is a refuge for our family whenever they need peace and solace. Our family has suffered many heartaches; illness, losses, upheavals in their life. Coming home to family in the Blessed House provides a place to regenerate and thrive with a strength that comes from the Lord.

Book III

Celebrations in Our Blessed House

CHAPTER 16
The Buttonwoods Resort

"Joann, try to hold Ethan still while I inject him with his insulin shot," I said as we struggled to restrain and inject her big-for-his-age three year old grandson. Here we were the grandmother and the out-of-practice nurse trying to take care of one autistic, diabetic child so his parents can have a few hours of vacation respite. We are not doing well.

"Don't let him fall asleep after lunch," his mother admonished before she left. Ethan fell asleep. We can not keep him awake. We consulted with my neighbor, Sue, who is also a nurse. She helped to allay our fears. We are so relieved to see his parents, Kim and Keith, return later in the day. Ethan survived his caretakers.

Joann is my youngest sister. She and I share the same mother but not a father. She lives in Ohio with her husband Frank. They have two children, Brian who recently married Missy and Kim who is married to Keith. Kim and Keith have two children, Cassidy, an exceptionally bright and sociable eight year old girl and Ethan, a handsome, lovable, autistic boy now six years old. My sister and her family have been vacationing at our home every July since our mother died fifteen years ago. As Joann's family propagated, our guest bedrooms filled to capacity. My sister tells her Ohio friends and family that she comes to her sister's Buttonwoods Resort every year on vacation. Summertime and holidays are prime time for guests. It's not unusual for us to have ten overnight family guests. I savor the companionship.

My sister loves to sit and relax in her favorite rocker and watch the changing tides and bobbing sailboats while feeling the warm sea breezes. We enjoy each others company and act like sisters who have lived together all our lives instead of fifteen years. Our brother Richard, who lives in R.I., visits often. Joann and Richard are similar, quiet, retiring homebodies who can communicate non-verbally.

Frank, my brother-in-law, and I compete in the kitchen; his specialty is sausage and peppers and tomato salad; mine is spaghetti and meatballs and linguini and clams. The family enjoys eating our Italian dishes. Keith and I do the quahogging. He is an avid fisherman and hunter of bears, deer and wild turkeys in Ohio. Keith's enthusiasm and helpfulness is contagious as he learns how to dig the quahogs and open them.

Ethan has to be watched at all times. Joann and Frank take turns playing and talking with him so that his parents can have a break from his constant challenges. Ethan is delighted with the beach; going in the water or sitting on the shore in his favorite chair. He requires food monitoring, testing and insulin shots twice a day. I commend Kim and Keith who have constant pleasant attitudes, patience, continuing knowledge and unconditional love to give to Ethan. His big sister, Cassidy, is a compassionate playmate. I admire the whole extended family who give their love, kindness, patience and support to him. Ethan is thriving and learning because of their fortitude and love. He is blessed to have such an extraordinary family. I am humbled and grateful to be part of their lives.

Our week-long celebration culminates with a seafood feast and live country music. A lobster dinner, a gift from our guests, is cooked by most of us. Our Ohio family's introduction to local seafood is a hit; steamers, quahogs, stuffies, clam chowder and lobster. Everyone gathers for this feast; our adult children who live in R.I., their spouses, girlfriends, boyfriends and children.

After dinner a melodious refrain is wafting along with the balmy summer breeze soothing our souls as we listen to Keith sing his own country love song to his wife. Keith and Kim are exchanging loving glances while he plays his guitar and sings for this rapt audience of many relatives. I am filled with an abundance of joy whenever I am cooking and entertaining family and friends. The Buttonwoods Resort is always open and usually full, all ten beds in five bedrooms, especially in the summertime and holidays! Our three grandchildren are frequent visitors.

Tom's Clam Chowder

One summer my son, Tommy, bought a used boat, moored it in front of our house and became a professional quahogger. He didn't make much money due to boat repairs but he enjoyed the experience and we enjoyed an abundance of quahogs. Many members of my family perfected various clam recipes together. This is my husband's Clam Chowder which he serves at our Family Reunions.

Saute in separate frying pan:
3 garlic cloves, minced
1 onion, chopped
2 stalks celery, cut up

Salt pork, cut up

In a large pan add equal amounts of clam juice and water.
Simmer 5-10 minutes.

Add the first four ingredients plus 2 lbs. cut up potatoes.
Add 2-3 shakes celery salt
1 T. Worcestershire sauce
2-3 shakes white pepper

When potatoes are done, add 1 quart of clams or large quahog meat.
Cook 5 minutes more.

CHAPTER 17
Grandma's Priceless Gifts

Camp Grandma

"Grandma, You be Charley Brown and I'll Be Snoopy. We'll sell Christmas wreaths just like they did on the video."

So, it began, another awesome day of play-acting with my creative amiable three year old grandson, Bobby.

The winter of 1990 was a mourning period for our family. Our youngest daughter Susan and her husband Bob were ending their five year marriage. The magnificent blossoming abundance of pink wild flowers that adorned our front yard during their joyous wedding reception have died beneath the cold winter snows. The lively rhythmic Caribbean music that urged us into wild dancing is silenced by the sadness in our hearts. The sparkling rippling waters at the edge of the lawn are now transformed into surging white-capped waves.

Our sadness melted away and our joy blossomed in the spring when their first child was born; my grandson Bobby. Summer has returned and I am singing love songs to my first grandchild.

"Grandma, let's play Nursery Rhymes. You read them and I'll be Jack be Nimble."

"Jack be Nimble, Jack Be Quick, Jack jumped over the candlestick." I read as Bobby jumpedover the candlestick; then bleated on all fours to 'Baa Baa Black Sheep' and later he flew out of the 'Blackbird's Pie'. I never knew babysitting could be so much fun. In the beginning, I changed his diapers, fed him a bottle and rocked him outside on the deck in the warm sunshine. My heart was bursting with love.

"Grandma, let's play Hide and Seek. I'll hide but don't look behind the kitchen door."

Every day that he came to my house while his mother was working was like opening presents on Christmas morning. I never knew what was in the package of playtime. I eagerly opened the presents and let him lead me to special places of the heart. It surprised me that I enjoyed our times together so much, after raising six children.

"Grandma, write it down, my poem. I'll tell you what to say."

After watching a video of Arthur and his friend writing rhyming poetry Bobby tried it. We filled a whole notebook full of whimsical rhyming poems before he could read or write. His laughter was contagious and we went on forever.

"Grandma, how old do I have to be before I can live in your house with 'the boys?'"

"Bobby, you live with your mother, in your own house."

"Grandma, I thought all 'the boys' live here, like Uncle Steve, Uncle Tommy and Uncle Dennis."

"Bobby, you can always come to visit."

Celebrating Christmas in our Blessed House every year with our extended family is a blend of holiness and playful camaraderie; Christmas

Mass, reading the Christmas Story, eating a special Italian dinner together and presenting our gifts to each other. One year Bobby added fun and games to Christmas.

"Grandma, let's hide some Christmas presents this year.
I'll help!"

"Bobby, where do you think we should hide them?"

"Grandma, how about the Porch, the Attic, the Garage, under the beds, everywhere."

"Bobby, should we give them clues?"

"Of course, Grandma. Let's write poems?"

"It's very cold
There is no heat
But if you go
You'll find a treat

You'll have to climb
To get your gift
When you see a blanket
Give it a lift."

Laughter and togetherness are the shining moments in our family.

"Grandma, I joined the Math Club after-school program.
I love math. It's fun!"

Our time together was shorter when Bobby began school. I picked him up after school and enjoyed his conversations about his friends, his teachers and schoolwork.

Grandma's Priceless Gifts multiplied along with my joy when Bobby was three years old. My son Michael and his wife Stephanie had a boy, Sean, energetic, friendly and loveable. I call him Nature Boy.

Nature Boy

"The only rule in my house is…

NO EATING ELECTRICAL CORDS*!"* A few months after his birth Sean arrived at the Blessed House with explicit babysitting instructions for me.

"Sean Michael Malone
The Manual."

This bright red professional manifesto began with the following:

"Preface
Please use this manual as a source of enjoyment and a guide to making things easy on you. Sean is an exceptionally adaptable baby with equally enjoyable disposition. Have fun this weekend."

My daughter-in-law Stephanie, a first-time, overcautious new mother is the author of this seven chapter manual. This is Sean's first trip without his parents, my son Michael and his wife Stephanie. I am delighted to care for our beautiful grandson whose smile warms me like sunshine.

THE MANUAL has me perplexed. Why am I being given instructions on how to care for a baby? Don't I have enough experience raising six children and babysitting for my first grandson? Are my methods antiquated? Is Sean so different? He looks happy and healthy to me but I'd better read 'THE MANUAL'.

"Chapter I—Emergency Numbers."

Listed are four numbers for the parents, as well as the Poison Control Center and Sean's pediatrician in Massachusetts. Okay, that's helpful if I need it.

"Chapter II—Sean's Sleeping Habits."

She lists seven 'Assistive Devices' to help Sean sleep. Scrawled across the bottom of every page in large black letters are...

"DO NOT LOOSE THE BINKY."

This is Assistive Device #1. Loose or lose?

"Assistive Device #4 Singing Hugh Little Baby in a high pitched voice."

I think I can sing my own lullaby.

Ending with...

"Caution: Unless he is crying hysterically or acting frightened try not to take him out of the crib. Try Assistive Device #1, 2, 4 and 7 before picking him up."

What is this all about? Do I really need seven Assistive Devices to put one baby to sleep? I always put my children in their crib and they shut their eyes and went to dreamland. Binky's were not even invented when his father was a baby.

"Chapter III—Sean's Eating Habits."

Timing, Amount, Temperature, Snacks and Table Food are expounded upon.

"His last meal, when I 'Top him off' is given around 8-8:30 p.m. The atmosphere is very important at this feeding because this is the feeding that should put him to sleep. I turn out all the lights and when he is finished with his bottle I put his Binky in his mouth.

Hmmm! I wonder if I'll have a problem putting Sean to sleep?

"Section IV—Diaper Changes
If he doesn't smell funky I change him every 2½ hours or so. I put the diaper on snug especially at night to prevent leaks. He likes it if you sing 'Ba Ba Ba Ba Ba Ba Butt Cream' to the tune of the TV series Batman. If he gives you a hard time during changes give him something off limits to play with. I usually tighten the diaper rash cream tube and give him that.

Changing Sean's diaper is a breeze. Imagine a throw-away diaper. I changed and washed hundreds of cloth diapers in my day. One time I had three babies in diapers at the same time. Oh, how I dreaded that diaper pail Can I sing my own tune to Sean? Will it work anyway?

"Section V—Sean's Likes
*For some odd reason Sean loves to go into the bathroom and get into the garbage basket. His favorite play things are electrical cords. The only rule in my house is…***NO EATING THE ELECTRICAL CORDS!!!**

The only rule…I have uncovered several rules in this manual. When can I relax and enjoy this contended bright baby?

"Section VI—Sean's Dislikes
Sean dislikes getting dressed, getting his face washed and waiting for food."

Sounds like he takes after my children. Food = #1 Priority in the Malone household. I do remember to feed the children first.

"Section VII—Misc. I Forgot About."

I could go on forever but it's so much fun just watching Sean that I put **'THE MANUAL'** away and took my cues from Sean. Stephanie was right, we did have so much fun together. Sean did not need Assistive Devices. He 'slept like a baby'.

This Manual and the enclosed Flo Chart with arrows going round and round highlight Stephanie's talents. She is an excellent Registered Nurse as well as a caring, loving mother who took the time to write her perceptions and aids on caring for her first child. Bravo Stephanie! I did have a few laughs and some suggestions were even helpful!"

"Sean Michael Malone

The Manual

Volume II."

"Sean, Sean, where are you?" No answer. Oh no, don't tell me I lost him. Stephanie and Mike will never forgive me. Where can he be? I search the house, walking upstairs to all five bedrooms, downstairs to the recreation room and back up to the kitchen, living room, library and all bathrooms.

"Sean, Sean." I scream as panic begins to set in. Did he wander off into the Bay waters? I walk outside.

"Hi Grandma. I was hungry."

Standing on the deck, covered in dark blue and purple stains from head to toe is my diaper clad two year old grandson eating mulberries. The mulberry tree is bursting with juicy purple berries and branches that overhang the deck for easy picking by Sean. My laughter explodes as I give my blue and purple Nature Boy a crushing hug. I am so relieved. My

Nature Boy loves mulberries and so do I. When we bought the house there was a small bush beside the house and thirty years later it stands 35 feet high with several smaller trunks. Despite cutting it back yearly, the berries continue to stain the deck, the furniture and the people every year in late June and early July. Everyone in the family wants to cut it down but Sean and I, the only mulberry lovers, protest. One year Stephanie climbed the tree and picked mulberries to make muffins for Sean. Speaking of Stephanie, thank the Lord I did not lose Sean or my grandmother babysitting privileges would be revoked.

Two years later Sean's sister Emily arrived, my first granddaughter.

"I think it's time to go to the hospital to have our baby, Mike." said Stephanie calmly. We are celebrating Tom and my 39th Wedding Anniversary around the table in the Blessed House. The hospital is 1 ½ hours away. Sean stayed with us and the next day we brought him to see his new sister, our anniversary granddaughter, a beautiful Angel from Heaven.

"Grandma, oh boy, now I have two kids to take care

of," sighed five year old Bobby.

I did not regularly babysit Emily and Sean as they lived an hour and one-half away but they visit every holiday and summertime.

Emily and I share a love for writing. She's had one poem published. We correspond regularly and I look forward to her hand drawn cards, drawings and original poetry.

A Halloween Card

An orange pumpkin, a black bat and a white ghost.

To Grandma From Emily

BOO

I love you.

Inside—To Grandma
Happy Halloween
Love, Goldilocks
Emily

A yellow haired girl with a pumpkin basket is surrounded by ghosts, goblins, pumpkins and a heart.

A Winter Card
> To PaPa and
> Grandma

A snowsuit and boot clad little girl stands next to a very tall squiggly snowman while covered with star shaped snow flakes.

> I am having fun. Are You?
> When are you coming?
> Love, Emily

Happy Birthday Grandma
> To #1 Grandma
> It's your Birthday all your wishes will come
> True. And I got this present for you!

> Colors because your like
> a rainbow! Sparkles because
> your as pretty as a butterfly!

*** Beads because your good great

at some things! A snap because

you just keep on trying!

Stripes because you look

great in them!

And a pretty

string just like

you.

From your favorite little girl!

The Birthday Gift

A thin silver chain holds

Beads . . . every shade of blue and green seen in the sea waters, most round, two flower shaped.

Charms . . . small and silver hanging from some of the beads, beach sandals, a dolphin, a beach chair and umbrella, a flamingo, an open clam shell with a pearl inside and an ivory fish.

Ivory Circles . . . with the names of our six children printed on them.

This charming, one-of-a-kind necklace is crafted by an artist and designed by my eight year old granddaughter Emily who captured two of my loves; my children and the sea.

Helen Keller said that the most beautiful things must be felt with the heart. My heart is thumping wildly as I sit at our dining room table in the Blessed House and behold our Anniversary granddaughter and her presents. I whisper a prayer of thanks to God who continues to send us His blessings . . . First Bobby, then Sean and now Emily! The fun goes on and on!

Camp Grandma

Visit any Season

For any Reason

That is the logo on my T-shirt that my grandchildren gave me. Every summer my three grandchildren come together at our seaside home for a week's vacation—no parents! I thought the cousins would enjoy playing together. I know I do. Bobby became the gentle guardian and patient teacher happy to be watching over his younger cousins; whether he is spreading suntan lotion on Sean's back before we go swimming, holding Emily's hand in the water, filling up the wading pool, teaching them to play ping-pong when they had to stand on milk crates to reach or giving Sean his outgrown golf clubs and golf lessons. He is also the peacemaker during brother and sister disagreements.

Our oldest daughter Cathleen, a teacher, joins us some years and challenges the children and me in new games. Skip-Bo and Rummikub are favorites, but Uno, Monopoly, Poker and Scrabble are prized also.

"Grandma, I can't paint seashells this year with two casts on my arms."

"Oh yes you can," said Sean and Emily, "we'll help you."

That was the summer Bobby had two broken arms racing in a dirt bike accident. My grandchildren showed me how loving, caring and compassionate they could be. Bobby has always shown great patience and caring for his cousins, now Emily and Sean began to shine. Emily mixed the paint on the brush and Sean placed the brush in Bobby's stiff fingers. Sean held the playing cards for Bobby. Emily held his cup to drink. They toasted his marshmallows and moved his Checkers. Sean placed the

Dominos and fed him a sandwich and together they towed the rubber boat with Bobby in it, careful not to splash. I treasure those colorful seashells.

The loving intimacy and fun my grandchildren share is like winning the lottery to me. The Lord sends many blessings on me, especially three grandchildren at Camp Grandma in the Blessed House. A friend of mine told me about an Italian saying: "Non Che Rosa Senza Spina."—There is no rose without thorns. My roses are healthy and blooming; Bobby is fifteen years old this summer, Sean, twelve years and Emily, ten years. At Camp Grandma, we put the world on pause and laugh and play. I hope this goes on forever. What blissful joy our grandchildren bring to our life.

Stuffies or Stuffed Quahogs

My grandchildren and I love to dig in the mud with our hands at low tide almost as much as we like eating steamers dipped in butter and baked Stuffies. My daughter Cathleen and I combined our cooking skills and this is our recipe.

When you open the quahogs, wash the shells and set them aside.
1 onion, chopped
2 green and 1 red pepper, chopped
1 stick margarine
2 garlic cloves, chopped
2 cups Italian seasoned bread crumbs
1 quart quahog meat

Saute onion, peppers and garlic in margarine until soft.

Add 3-5 shakes of Worcestershire sauce.

Add 2 teaspoons mustard.

Mix in the 2 cups of seasoned bread crumbs.

Simmer for 10 minutes.

Add chopped quahogs and simmer another 5 minutes.

Fill the open shells with this mixture.

Bake in 350 degree oven for 20 minutes.

Soft Shell Clams or Steamers

This is Sean's favorite.

Steam the clams with onion slices and pepper flakes until the shells open.

Serve as an appetizer with melted butter and clam juice for dipping.

CHAPTER 18
Who Stole the Birthday Candelabra?

"Ladies and Gentlemen, Welcome to the Malone Mystery Night Dinner Theater under the Big Top," bellowed Jack, the stately coiffured, Ringmaster, dressed in his brass buttoned jacket and silk cravat.

"Tonight we will solve the mystery of the stolen Birthday Candelabra. Then, we will have a special sixtieth birthday celebration for Tom, Norm and me. You will be given many clues but do not be deceived or derailed. Be alert! It could be Biggo—the Strong Man or the sly Gypsy Lady or maybe Calculating Cowboy Norm."

Birthdays are major events in our family. We celebrate by inviting all family members to our home to dine on the Birthday person's favorite dinner and cake that I take pleasure in cooking. My proudest accomplishments are my marriage and our six children. This calls for rejoicing. The first birthday we toasted after moving into our Blessed House was our youngest Susan's fourteenth birthday. She was born in a snowstorm in the early hours after Valentine's Day. Many of our family birthdays are held around holidays. Our son Dennis was born just after

Easter Sunday, the day before his father's birthday. Cathleen, our first child exploded on the scene on the fourth of July and I was born on Thanksgiving.

One momentous occasion was my husband Tom and our close friends Jack and Norm's sixtieth birthday event. We invited forty of our friends to a Mystery Night dinner theater party. As each guest arrived they selected which room in our house they would like to be in to solve the mystery. Will it be the Columbo Room, our Library-Office Room, the Hercule Poirot Room, the central Great Room; the Inspector Maigret Room, our breezy screened porch or the Miss Marple Room, our upstairs bedroom-sitting room?

"Take your drink and hors d'oeuvres folks and follow a Circus Character to your room. Follow the clues carefully and when you solve the puzzle come back under the Big Top," directed the smooth-tongued Ringmaster.

This improvisational play has no script, no rehearsals, just clues and characters. The latter did not need them. The cast took on a life of their own when they donned their costumes. Carol, an unpretentious woman astonished us with her great act as the quick-witted seductive Gypsy Lady, dancing around in her scarves and acres of bangles. Marge, the Trapeze Artist looks fantastic in her blue satin clinging speedo jumpsuit and long Dolly Parton wig.

"Is that really your hair?" someone asked. Marge did not have to act, just sashay around looking sexy and giving orders.

"I didn't do it. Make sure you don't vote for me. I was practicing my charms on my friendly snakes," offered Karon, the fake tattooed Snake Lady.

"You might want to look at Tom Biggo the Strong Man. He's covering up something with that smirking Irish face," suggested Gypsy Lady Carol. We were interrupted by a commotion on the front lawn as Calculating Cowboy Norm dressed in his black ten-gallon hat and my vest burst into the room, "Follow me, follow me," he ordered! "There is a disturbance outside. Maybe they found the Birthday Candelabra!" On the front lawn, Ron and Bill, dressed in tight black sweats and shoeless are doing a believable high wire tightrope act with a balancing broom, a tiny red tricycle and a rope that is flat on the ground.

"Marvelous! Fantastic! Can you believe it?" exclaimed the crowd standing along the railing on the front deck. We are all awed by this spectacular improvisation.

Guests disperse into the four Detective Rooms. The amateur sleuths do not need coaxing. Imbibed with clues and spirits, animated discussions are reverberating throughout the house. When sated we gather together in the Great Room.

"We voted for the Snake Lady. She looks sneaky," shouted the guests from the Miss Marple Room.

"No, it's Calculating Cowboy Norm. He's trying to distract us," disagreed the Columbo Room guests.

"Inspector Maigret's Room votes for the debonair Ringmaster. He had access to the Candelabra."

"You are all wrong. Our clever detective work in the Hercule Parrot Room insists it is Marge, the Trapeze Artist. She tried to cover up but we detect she is wearing a wig and is really the notorious Bonnie!"

No one guessed who really robbed the non-existent Birthday Candelabra.

Finale—Ron and Bill, the Tight Rope Artists, looking guilty, enter carrying a makeshift candelabra. They held it high in the air for everyone to see. I was surprised to recognize my three bulb brass porch floor lamp minus the lamp shade, but what we really see is a three pronged Birthday Candelabra.

"Bravo! Bravo!" we cry out.

Dinner—Everyone eating with relish my Italian specialties of Meatballs, Sausage and Lasagna, as well as a pot-pourri of hot food contributed by the guests. The Lord has blessed us with many friends. While singing Happy Birthday to Tom, Jack and Norm and eating their birthday cake, I am reminded of what's important in our life; reaching out to long-lasting friends and having fun!

Encore—Blessings from the Lord continue through the night. A full moon is lighting up the deck as we strengthen our friendships at the Blessed House while enjoying the balmy summer breezes and spectacle of the full moon shining on the water that the Lord proved for us tonight.

Book IV

Friends—Just Like Family

CHAPTER 19
Barbara, Beer, and Bulging Bikini

"Grab the beer cans before they sink Barbara," they shouted at me as I struggled to free myself from underneath our capsized sunfish boat.

It was a beautiful sunny, warm, windy late June day. I had just put a chicken in the oven when my friend, Jack, arrived at our beach house with his sunfish and John to launch his boat from my beach. Jack and his wife, Marcy, are long time neighborhood friends. He is a principal at John Green School. John is a principal at Oakland Beach School where I worked briefly as a school nurse.

"Would you like to come for a sail with us." asked Captain Jack. I was thrilled at the offer. I loved sailing almost as much as I loved swimming. I'm always ready for an adventure on the sea. I changed into my bikini bathing suit almost as fast as I said yes.

We carried the boat and the beers to the water. I was reveling in the idyllic sail sitting atop a crowded two person sunfish listening to the two sun-glassed, hatted principals banter. The hilarity was catching as we laughed and bounced along with the waves. It wasn't until we had sailed to the middle of Greenwich Bay that my senses picked up some off-beat vibes. John let go of the line and it was trailing in the water. We could not steer the boat without a secure line. They haggled about who was going to jump off the boat and tie the line.

"You're the Captain, Jack, you should go." said John.

"You jump John, you let go of the line." he countered. The affable exchange volleyed back and forth endlessly. I knew I was not volunteering to jump off, tread water, tie a line and shimmy back onto the boat. I waited patiently while we drifted along. This conversation revealed to me that they had been celebrating a Last Day of School Principal's Party before they came to my house. It was apparent now that they had imbibed a few beers before the sail. Jack finally jumped into the water to retrieve the line and John and I laughed heartily when Jack landed on a sandbar and was standing in waist deep water.

Mission accomplished we continued our erratic fun ride. Our sails full of wind we blew across the water closer to East Greenwich Yacht Club where the elite dock their yachts. After an abrupt tack, we came-about, capsized and plunged under the water. I heard my instructions from Captain Jack as I crawled and gasped my way out from under the sail.

"Grab the beer cans before they sink, Barbara. Forget about the hats and sunglasses." Fortunately I did not wear any that day. I swam around frantically collecting as many beer cans as I could.

"We'll upright the boat," Jack called. With the boat still submerged I had no where to put the cans so I began stuffing them into the bottom of my bathing suit. I ran out of room so next I stuffed my already full bikini top with several more beer cans. In the meantime I'm treading water waiting for the boat to be righted up. Eventually the boat surfaced and they pulled me up into the boat with my beer laden bikini bulging all over.

I was the heroine of the day. I received much praise and no one mourned the loss of sunglasses and hats.

We had a hilarious time, sans alcohol on my part, and were in a jovial mood when we arrived back at my house. Tom was waiting on the hill, home from work, waiting and watching this noisy skirmish, trying to bring the boat up the hill and onto the trailer. I bubbled over telling Tom about our Principals' Last Day Party sail on the water. He smiled a little, knowing my love for the sea until we went into the house and smelled the burnt chicken dinner. What a great day I had! I'm so lucky to have a house so close to the sea and friends to take me sailing and back home safely.

What a fun place to live!

Friends—Just like Family! That is a banner I would hang in the Blessed House. The more we give, the more we receive. Sharing our blessings with friends is like finding a treasure chest of gold. Many times the treasure is a gathering of friends at the Blessed House cooking a clam bake in the rocks on our sandy beach, or eating dinner of spaghetti and meatballs, sometimes celebrating holidays and non-holidays. The Lord's blessings follow us when we have adventures with our friends sailing or traveling.

The Brosco's dazzled us with the thrill of viewing America's Cup races in Newport aboard their classic fifty foot wooden boat, Spray.

Marcy and Jack graduated from a two man Sunfish to a twenty-nine foot sailboat called Green Eyes.

"Jump, Marcy, Jump," yelled Captain Jack. Marcy hesitated.

"Jump, you have to tie the line," he urged. Marcy jumped.

"Splash!" She landed down in the water between their boat and the dock. Jack jumped onto the dock and pulled his drenched wife out of the water. Tom scurried to secure their boat to the dock. Marcy, fully-clothed, drips water from her hair down to her shoes. She is not amused. We stifle our laughter until it brews and bursts!

Sailing, sunning, eating and camping out in Newport aboard their boat, as well as in the Blessed House, forged our friendships while giving us many hours of laughter and pleasure.

CHAPTER 20
The Apprentice First Mate

"Barbara, how would you like to go sailing to Newport with me this weekend?" my friend Karon asked.

"Great, I love sailing on the LaJournada. Who else is coming?" I asked.

"Just you and me. We'll have a fabulous time, a women's weekend. We'll moor at the upscale Ida Lewis Yacht Club, and walk into town for dining and shopping.

"But Karon, I don't know how to sail a boat. I'm not a sailor, just a lazy passenger watching you and Bill and my husband, Tom, do all the work.

"We can do anything the men can do," she emphasized. "You can be my first mate. It's easy, I'll tell you what to do!"

We set sail from East Greenwich Yacht Club early in the morning on a clear sunny day in August. I was filled with anticipation and apprehension. We have been on many journeys to Newport on Karon and Bill's twenty-eight foot Columbia sailboat but this is our first solo sail.

"Barbara, pick an object straight ahead and steer the boat while I put up the sails," she said as she walked to the bow of the boat undoing the line and releasing the jib sail. She repeated this with the mainsail, both times securing the lines in an exact cris-cross pattern. Wow, I thought, I have the easy role. This is going smoothly as there are only a few boats and a large body of water in Greenwich Bay. I am feeling more confident. Karon took over the steering and we waved to my family who were watching us from our deck opposite Sally Rock Point and sailed on. The house looked so pretty from this view. I was luxuriating in the serenity of this peaceful sail as we bobbed along on the gentle swells. The cooling breezes ripped across my skin tenderly.

"Hard-to-Lee-Coming About," yelled Karon. Time to tack or turn the boat. We are sailing into Narragansett Bay now. Tacking is a little more complicated. As Karon released the line on one side of the boat I ducked under the boom and secured the line in the cris-cross pattern on the other side. We had to move quickly, shifting the sail, but on such a perfect sailing day with enough wind to fill our sails I felt no pressure, yet. We passed Prudence and Jamestown Islands steering clear of quahog boats and lobster traps. The journey takes about three and one-half to five hours sailing from East Greenwich Yacht Club to Newport, depending on the wind. The pressure began to build as we sailed past the Newport Naval Base where a huge battleship was moored, on our approach to the Newport Bridge and harbour beyond it.

"Barbara, we have to tack again. Get ready. Hard-to-Lee-Coming About," she said in her Captain's voice. I responded to that command as my heart started pumping adrenaline. I was staring

at the tall steel piers that hold up the Newport Bridge that appeared ominously in front of us. We are depending on the wind to push us through the middle and we are going sideways, tacking to catch the wind.

I held my breath and prayed as Karon expertly navigated the LaJournada between the piers and under the bridge. I breathed a sigh of relief briefly, but my night-mare was just about to begin.

Newport harbour on a weekend in August is a massive moving traffic jam. Motor boats and motoring sailboats of all sizes are everywhere; coming in, going out and zigzagging across. Even a five-story cruise ship is anchored off shore. Many boats are heading to yacht clubs, docks, and moorings that surround this crescent shape harbour. Some boats are cruising looking at the scenery; Fort Adams, Hammersmith Farm (Jackie's O's former place), Castle Hill and the twelve-meter yachts. Windsurfers are darting closely across our bow with ease. There are no traffic lights, no traffic cops, no stop signs and no white line to follow. All sailors are on their own!

My anxiety didn't erupt until Karon told me I had to climb up on the bulkhead, release and secure the line and lower and furl the mainsail, alone.

"Oh, no," I cried.

"Barbara, I have to steer the boat because of all this traffic," she explained. I panicked and didn't move.

Karon shouted in her Captain's voice. "Barbara, get up there now! We have to motor in or we'll have a collision. Move!" I tried but I was so frightened to stand up with the strong gusts of wind that I crawled on my hands and knees up onto the rough bulkhead and grasped the mast with a death grip.

"Barbara, let go of that mast and undo the line. Do it on your knees, if you have to," she bellowed. I heard Karon but my fingers were having a difficult time undoing the tight line. "I can't undo it," I yelled into the wind. "You have to do it Barbara, or you will have to come here and steer the boat," she screamed. That frightened me even more so I struggled and eventually lowered and furled the mainsail. When I finished I crawled to the cockpit and collapsed in a stupor. My knees were rubbed raw.

"Good job, Barbara. I knew you could do it, she said in her friendly voice. As she motored into the harbour she radioed ahead, "LaJournada calling Ida Lewis Yacht Club, seeking permission to anchor." She received a go-ahead and an escort to our mooring next to the yacht club. Karon secured the boat. I didn't stop shaking until after our vodka cocktails. We were celebrating our accomplishment when we discovered our friends Ed and Fran moored close by. They invited us on their sailboat. The club had a private party and was playing lively music. The four of us sang and danced and drank on their twenty-eight foot sail boat; having a good time. I didn't realize how good a time we had until I saw pictures later of our evening together. Karon and I are draped across Ed, each with a half-empty bottle, gin and vodka. The glaze in our eyes and the windblown hairdo gave me a clue that we must have had a wild night.

I will sail again with Karon and I will even stand up next time, and we did with less anxiety and more playfulness. You never know what you can do unless you try.

CHAPTER 21
Hair and Humor

The Merry-Go-Round and The Brillo Pad

"Honey, who fried your hair with that permanent?" asked a new hairdresser on a recent visit. She was running her fingers through my short, curly hair as I tried to speak. She rambled on, "Honey, would you like me to try to cut off this dreadful permanent?"

"No," I gasped. "That's my natural curl!" "Oh." she said quietly.

"I would like highlighting, to cover my gray hairs."

I have been riding the Merry-Go-Round for years; around and around I go, always ending up in the same place. Each round I try to catch the Brass Ring but it always eludes me. My Brass Ring is straight hair!

I was born with kinky, bushy, curly light brown hair, lots of it. It's always been impossible to put a comb through it. When I first hopped on the Merry-Go-Round I tried plastering my unruly curls down with various kinds of hair grease, like Brill Creme. My childhood was spent in pigtails. Everyone had straight hair. As I grew older I did not want to be different. I rode round and around with giant rollers, curling irons, flat

153

irons, hair-thinning cremes, mouses and conditioners. I could not catch the Brass Ring and ended up in the same place as I started. My curls popped up indiscriminately.

My friends would put their hands on my hair and exclaim, "Even though it looks like a King Size Brillo Pad it feels soft." I guess that was a compliment. A hairdresser regularly "thinned." my hair. One year I even wore a blond straight page-boy style wig. No one knew me. My classmates in my adult college classes flirted with me, thinking I was a new student.

During the hippy era of the sixties I abandoned my quest for straight hair. I cut my hair into a very bouffant Afro hairdo and went with the flow. "The Barbershop is open. Who would like to be first?" I ask as I assemble my tools, barber scissors, comb, and wastebasket in the kitchen of the Blessed House. I was the barber in my family for myself, my silky curly-haired husband and six curly-haired children. I had no training, just experience, cutting my own hair for years. I cut three sons' hair into Afros also. We happened to have our only formal family portrait taken at this time. The Afro picture hangs on the wall next to the 'Phyllis Diller' one in our home. It has provided many laughs in the family as our sons and daughters marry and have children.

One year on a trip to St. Martin I came closer and closer to the Brass Ring and I, a curly-haired Italian, provided more amusement to my Irish husband and our two Irish friends, the Murphys. Having a sense of humor is a very significant value in the Irish culture. We were sitting on our balcony overlooking the clear blue-green Caribbean waters. We had left demanding careers and eleven children back in oblivion. We were experiencing the first joys of liberation and libation.

We lingered over our lunch of pungent Island cheeses, spicy dry sausages and fresh crusty home-made bread washed down with an abundance of Merlot Wine. When I was sated and could no longer delay my desirous urges to swim and let this warmth inside my body meld with my skin outside, I left the group and went swimming. They were engaged in talking and savoring more wine.

My body tingled with delight. My pleasure continued to swell when I saw a raft about two hundred feet from shore. I decided to swim to the raft feeling confident that I could hoist my thirty-five year old, out-of-shape body up onto the raft. As I approached the raft two Adonis-like young men jumped up and each held out a hand to help me. Like a synchronized ballet they touched my fingertips, flipped over my head in unison, dove into the sea and swam away, while I plunged into the depths of the water. When I surfaced, struggling, spitting and stunned I climbed onto the raft and lay down to breathe and unwind.

Convinced that the imbibing Irishmen had not seen this fiasco, I was quiet when I returned.

"Did you have a good swim?" one asked. "Yes," I answered. "How was the water?" "Very nice and warm," I replied. "Anything unusual happen?" they persisted. "No," I said stoically. Finally, "Barbara, why did you throw those two helpful men into the water?"

When they couldn't contain themselves any longer they simultaneously burst out laughing raucously. I did not share their laughter, then. Instead I gave them my version of the Evil Eye! Maybe you had to be Irish!

Later that evening we attended a Native Festival. We were the only four white persons among the four hundred natives at the fairgrounds. Loud Calypso music and steel drums were playing on an outdoor stage, delicious foreign smells of food came from the booths and everyone was dancing. We were hesitant but curious and soon joined in the engaging festivities. Most of the natives were wearing dark wool ski-caps in this ninety degree weather. I began asking questions to a young man.

"Why do you wear that winter hat?"

"Ma'am, this hat holds down the kink and the frizz of my hair," he replied.

I was intrigued. "Is that all you do? I really need help."

"Go to the market and buy this 'Kinky-No-More' cream and use it daily and wear a wool cap to bed at night." he advised. I was so excited. I was getting close. The next day I saturated my hair with 'Kinky-No-More'. When we went out that evening with our friends I was elated. My hair was straight and smooth at last even though it was vile-smelling. 'Ping! Ping!' We were sitting at an outdoor café having dinner and could not figure out where the sound was coming from. 'Ping! Ping! "My dinner partners noticed one curl after another popping out of my head like springs. By the end of the evening the Brass Ring receded and the kinky curls were in full swing. My husband and friends smiled, snickered and then launched into a full belly laugh. This time I joined them.

I would not be defeated. I went to a professional hairdresser to straighten my hair; a very expensive reverse permanent. It was not permanent and lasted only a month but I persisted and returned later for another treatment.

"Are you sure you want me to straighten your hair again?" asked the hairdresser.

"See the man sitting next to you, he's paying me to put curls in his hair, so his straight hair can look just like yours."

That was the last time I reached for the Brass Ring. I stopped the Merry-Go-Round and embraced my Brillo Pad and loved my kinky curls that God and my Italian ancestors gave me.

CHAPTER 22
Wednesday Women's Sail and Their Secret

As we sailed by Sally Rock Point, a marker in the Greenwich Bay, directly across from my water-front home, we crashed into another sailboat. Crunch!

Karon, my best friend, and her husband Bill were both experienced Captain's of their boat, the La Journada. I am a novice sailor who has sailed on many adventures alone, with Karon, many times from East Greenwich to Newport, a four to six hour sail depending on the wind. One summer Karon, a dynamic, outspoken, generous woman invited seven women, inexperienced sailors, for Wednesday evening sails. I usually worked on Wednesday and did not join the group, except once, on that fateful evening.

We were sailing back to the East Greenwich Yacht Club after a delightful two hour sail around Greenwich Bay, reaching around to Rocky Point. The boat was filled with laughter, talking, eating gourmet hors d'oeuvres and taking turns at the helm. There was only one other sailboat on the wide expanse of water when we crashed head-on. The chattering women were silenced. Karon took the wheel on our boat as the all-male crew slid by on the damaged boat swearing profusely at us. They continued their swearing as they sailed away in the opposite direction. We cowered knowing that we were at fault. The large mainsail obscured the 'novice Captain' at the wheel's view, at that time. The lookout was not watching. There were no holes in our boat, just the paint scraped off the starboard side. Karon turned into the wind, we dropped the sails and she motored silently into port.

By the time we spotted our mooring, the black night had descended on us. Our distressed Captain began barking orders. "Joan, hold the spotlight steady and find the mooring." Barbara, get the boat hook and grab the mooring and secure it." I had done this before but never in the spotlighted dark night. Karon motored the boat as close as she could and I leaned over the boat with the boot hook but the mooring eluded me. The Captain was angry because now she had to motor in a wide arc all around the mooring in between other moored sailboats. I tried to hook it again, reaching into the dark water with the long poled boat hook. I missed again. "Dammit! Someone else try to get it and hurry up or we will miss the last launch to take us into shore," Karon yelled. Silence prevailed as two more women tried and failed as Karon continued to motor around in a circle each time. Her frustration level rose and her anger erupted. "Barbara, this is your last try. Hang over the side of the boat and catch that mooring with your hands," she screamed at me. "Joan, you grab one of her legs, Ellen, you grab her other leg, Eileen you hang onto her middle and hurry up." I was in shock. I couldn't believe I was hanging over the side of the boat completely upside down with three women hanging onto me. I was one of the heavier women but I had more experience. I prayed that I would catch the mooring before the women's arms tired. Ah, success! I hooked us up and the women unhooked me and I was relieved momentarily, until sparks began to fly and it looked like fireworks on the stern of the boat. Someone had thrown the anchor on top of the motor. We were fearful a fire would break out. The Captain cursed as all of us women fled quickly to the bow of the boat ready to jump in the water if we had to abandon ship. Karon turned off the motor, gave three blasts on her air horn and the launch came and carried away a quiet, subdued group of women. No fire erupted. Karon was frightened that Bill would find out about the crash.

We were in a football huddle in the dimly lit parking lot sharing her game plan-secrecy about the incident. Our talk was interrupted by a group of five angry men coming ashore who said to us, "Did you see a boat come in with a bunch of ditzy women in it? They crashed into us. We can't believe it. They had the whole Bay to sail in, with no other boats in sight and we had the right-of-way. Our boat was damaged."

"No, we didn't see anything," we muttered in unison. As we all rushed to our cars to drive home we heard them yell "We're going to keep looking for them." The Wednesday Women's group never betrayed their secret to anyone. That was their last sail that summer.

I was in prison and you visited me.

CHAPTER 23
Lethal Storms

Sometimes life is not fair!

"All Buttonwoods residents must evacuate." came the order. Our family stampedes into adrenaline alert. Deck furniture, garbage cans, potted plants, umbrellas and beach chairs are whisked into the garage. Large sheets of plywood are nailed against the myriad of windows.

"There may be major flooding if the storm surge comes at high tide."

We transfer all moveable valuable objects from the first floor of the house to third floor bedrooms, especially my 25 family picture albums and hand-crocheted afghans. Hurricane Bob is crashing into R.I. with 90 to 100 mile an hour winds in August 1984. Trees crash and electrical wires swing like jump ropes. It is our first hurricane in the Blessed House. Most of us journey inland to stay with family or friends. My husband Tom and son Steve decide to wait out the storm in the boarded-up house. Listening to the roaring winds that sound like a speeding train out of control on the rooftop, they have second thoughts about staying.

"Let's see what it's like outside."

Stepping onto the front deck they are awed by the power of nature. The seas are churning with white-cap frosting, trees are bending, a forgotten red sand pail on the beach becomes a projectile and a cold misty spray washes over them.

"Dad, I think it's time to leave. We've done all we can to secure the house," screamed Steve into the wind.

"Let's go," Tom quickly agreed.

Hurricane Bob is hammering the coastline. The winds are blasting the Marina on our Bay where four feet waves loosen many yachts from their moorings and crash them into the rocky shoreline. The LaJournada, our friends Karon and Bill's boat is ravaged.

Returning home, after the storm, we snake our way down our street dodging tree limbs intertwined with electrical wires and debris. Pulling into the driveway the sight of our Blessed House unscathed in this tumult sends loud prayers of thanksgiving up into the heavens. The Lord spared our Blessed House from the wrath of Hurricane Bob. The old swamp maple tree, the tulip tree and the mulberry tree are standing tall minus some leaves. The only damage is to the arborvitae hedge which eventually dies from the whipping salt spray. Surprisingly, there is little erosion on the beach this time. As we remove the plywood from the windows we inadvertently tear two 6 ft. screens. Electricity and phone lines are out and won't be restored for a week.

"Tom, I'm so glad you had the gas grille built into the house. I can cook our meals but refrigeration is going to be a problem."

"Don't worry. Our family is safe and our home is safe. I think I can deal with ice."

We do mourn for the loss of Karon and Bill's boat. Saying goodbye brings to mind many joyful memories.

"I'm going to miss the lazy weekends camping with our friends on the boat in Newport, especially when the Tall Ships came into the harbour. Karon and Bill are so much fun and so generous," I said.

"You also enjoyed swimming off the boat, Barbara. My favorite time was the cocktail hour," joined in Tom.

"Remember the time we sailed to Block Island and it rained? We still had a great time. That was when I had that long sea-sick ride home and I was so relieved when our house appeared on the starboard side of the boat because I knew we were almost home."

Tom voiced out loud what we were both thinking. "I wonder if they will buy a new boat."

This storm and yachting disaster is minor compared to the unknown storm that is brewing and will surface with a vengeance.

"The wind is blowing at 25 knots. It is perfect for wind surfing," said Bill who stands on our front lawn with his anometer held high in the wind. The decision is made. Bill and Karon will not replace their sailboat, The LaJournada. A new sport begins. Bill arrives with several sails, a board, a harness and a wet suit and begins to assemble all the pieces for windsurfing on our front lawn. Everyone is fascinated with his tedious process of measuring the wind, unrolling and selecting the proper sail for the intensity of the wind. Karon brings a gourmet picnic lunch of homemade salads, sandwiches and drinks. Several of their family members came also. When Bill is ready, both families sit in the lawn chairs at the edge of the water eagerly awaiting this new spectacle.

After only two attempts Bill balances himself on the board, tugs at the rope, grasps the sail-bar and raises the wind sail. He glides gracefully with the wind currents that take him into deeper waters on Greenwich Bay like a seagull taking flight.

"Wow," shouts the chorus of aspiring wind-surfers. We are not surprised at Bill's athletic prowess. He is a tennis champion, marathon runner, swimmer as well as a competent sailor. As an athlete Bill eats healthy meals, doesn't smoke, and exercises every day.

We are so happy to share our Blessed House and waters with our friends. Comraderie and merriment among families are enriching our friendships. We watch Bill teach his two sons, my two sons and his son-in-law how to master the windsurfing techniques in subsequent weeks.

"You need strong arm and leg muscles and an abundance of patience for pulling, standing, turning and balancing on this slender board. When you grip the sail-bar hold on tight," Bill instructs his proteges. There are many attempts that end with the boys' splashing into the water. We laugh when my sons, Mike and Steve, mount the board and dunk into the water repeatedly. We admire the persistence of those who succeed.

"This is not as easy as it looks," mumbles my son Mike.

"Keep trying," shouts our chorus of cheerleaders. Swimming in the Bay is the alternate choice of sport for many family members.

Tom and I are rich with many valuable antiques—our old friends. Karon and Bill are precious and rare. They are here when we need them, for work or pleasure. When we were preparing to have my daughter Susan's wedding reception on the front lawn of the Blessed House, they arrived ready to work.

"What can we do to help you?"

We did not realize how much work it was to plan, order, self-cater, pick up food as well as decorate for 150 expected guests. Karon and Bill added much needed organization. They labored in the kitchen preparing and cutting up cheese hors d'oeuvres. They also brought their son to serve guests at the Seafood Station during the reception. Anytime I need Karon or Bill for a large party or small gathering at the Blessed House, they are our helpmates.

"Barbara, is the wind up?" comes the familiar call from Bill for the next several summers. I thought it would never end.

Sometimes life is not fair! Bill died after a brief illness of pancreatic cancer at 60 years old. I still see Bill gliding along on the Bay waters when the wind is up.

Several years later the winter winds and rising tides caused extensive damage to our beach washing away fifty feet of land. After three years of negotiating for a permit to build a wall we are ready to repair the damage from several winter storms.

The experts have ben consulted and this is the only solution. Our two neighbors to the left of us will continue the wall onto their property. The cost is monumental! We have no choice.

Beach chairs line the top of the grassy cliff behind the yellow construction tape as we watch the monster machines, dump trucks and steam shovels maneuver on the beach. A steady stream of booted, sweat-soaked men hauled the dumped rocks around the shore line. For three noisy summer and fall months this was the gathering place for family, friends and neighbors. We stared at the precise cutting and laying of the black fabric which will hold the sand in place. We shouted to hear each other and continued to ogle as the rocks crawl slowly up the hill forming a retaining wall.

"Job well done
Erosion is forestalled
I will live on."

The house whispers to me.

CHAPTER 24
Bizarre Bedfellows

There I stood, naked as a newborn, alone, in a strange hotel room in N.Y. City when I heard the key turn in the lock of the door.

We are on our annual visit to the big city to kick up our heels, eat in elegant restaurants, dance in exotic nightclubs, experience the Broadway Theater and enjoy our long-lasting friendships with the Murphys and Daleys. Relax Restore Rejuvenate—That's our mission. We left behind our work, our worries and several young children being cared for by grandparents. We drove three and one-half hours from R.I. in two cars inviting other friends, the Mallorys, to join us this year. The Fitzgeralds will be arriving at the hotel later in the day.

"I don't know if I can handle this! This is too nerve-wracking." exclaimed Tim Mallory as he paced the lobby floor while his eyes darted all around the room.

"Tim, relax, don't look so suspicious. I'll check in and Joan and you can share our room," explained my husband, Tom.

"You mean I have to sneak up the back stairs to your room so no one will see me, just to save a few bucks?" he inquires.

"Hey, Tim, we're all trying to save a few bucks. We're sharing with the Daleys," joined in Dick.

"We can do it," interrupts his wife Joan. "Just follow me."

After settling into our room we decided to change into our bathing suits and go for a swim in the roof top pool. My husband went to check on the Daley's and Murphy's accommodation in theroom next to us and tell them our plans. Joan went into the bathroom to change. Tim was sitting near the door staring into space.

"I'll change into my bathing suit in the adjoining room since the Fitzgeralds won't be here until later," I said. When I heard the unexpected key in the lock I panicked. I didn't know what to do or where to go! Instinctively I covered my eyes with both my hands and stumbled blindly into our room, leaving my clothes behind on the floor. Giggles erupted in me as I stood stripped, senseless and sightless for several minutes. When my giggles burst into hysterical laughter I threw myself down prone onto the nearest bed. I could not stop laughing. They tell me Tim was in shock staring with his mouth wide open. Then Joan came out of the bathroom. "What's going on out here?" she asked. No answer, just more laughter. "What's the matter with her?" questioned Joan but Tim was mute. She came over to the bed and twisted the bedcover over my naked body. When my husband arrived he calmed me down and we all had a good laugh, or so I thought.

Later that evening, we dined at Top of the Sixes, a rooftop restaurant with spectacular views of the city. Then, we danced and drank our way through a few nightclubs. About one o'clock in the morning I was dragging, so was Tim. We couldn't party any longer.

"I'm going back to the hotel room. I don't want to spoil anyone else's fun. You can go on without me," I said. Tim seconded the motion.

My husband said, "That will save me a trip. Tim can accompany you back to the room and we can continue on our way."

"Oh no, he won't." piped up Joan. "I'll go back to the room with them."

My husband pleaded, "Joan, you don't have to go. You're not tired, stay with us. Barbara falls asleep as soon as her head hits the pillow." Joan came back to the hotel room and sat stoically in the dark while Tim and I in our respective beds immediately fell asleep.

That was the last time, after this trip, that any of us ever saw the Mallorys again. Several months later, we heard that Tim and Joan had divorced. I thought we were all having a good time!

CHAPTER 25
The Irish Brotherhood

Highlights of a two-week road trip in Ireland from five Irish Rovers and one Italian, Jack & Carol, Dick & Helen, Tom & Me!

Carol
Connor's Pass

We almost lost Jack, Carol's husband, over the side of the mountain. We are driving through Connor's Pass, the only way to get to the old-time seaside village of Dingle. Our unwieldy bulky twelve passenger van is climbing the mountain and clinging to the narrow winding road with five passengers and Tom in the driver's seat. We stop the van at a lookout and enjoy a stunning panoramic view of purple flowered mountains and multi-colored green valleys.

"That bell shaped purple flower is what they make the drug Digitalis from. It used to be used as a heart medication," Helen relates. We feast our eyes on the wondrous sight of the patch work quilted valley with shades of green from lemon yellow to deep hunter green. The quilt is formed in squares and rectangles, divided by stone walls or dark brush. A few plots have houses, some cows, sheep, goats and horses but others are smooth as a meadow. Dark clouds put the mountain top in shadows of purple, gray and green. Yellow buttercups, pink rhododendrums, red bleeding hearts and graceful white calla lilies climb the mountain.

Mesmerized by the view we do not see Jack take a step backward and almost fall into a deep ravine with a fast-running stream.

"Help, help," Carol yells as she grabs Jack's arm. We all haul Jack back to safety, count our blessings and continue driving up the dangerous mountain. We climb higher and higher into a smoky mist that is embracing the mountain. Haunting celestial harp music envelops us in mystery.

"Tom, I think you drove too far. We're in heaven a little too early," said Carol as we giggle in unison. On the mountain top a young Irish lad is playing heavenly harp music surrounded by hushed tourists. We are speechless and motionless as this peaceful spiritual experience permeates our body and soul.

Dingle Bay

We are jolted back to reality as we descend the mountain slowly dodging cars, sheep, bicycles and hikers. Walking around the small picturesque village at the waters edge is worth the trip. On the road again our mission is to drive around Dingle Bay. Wow! We are not prepared for a hair-raising stress-filled narrow road around the mountain overlooking choppy waters hundreds of feet below. When our hearts settle back to a regular rhythm we are undecided about the return trip.

"I think we should follow this lane in the mountain," suggested Jack.

"Jack, this looks like a goat path," said Dick.

"It's better than going back to that menacing road."

We did not see any goats but we met a farmer and his dog trying to get his sheep out of the lane in front of our van. We stopped abruptly. Our hearts did not rest as this narrow dirt lane away from Dingle Bay was definitely designed for mountain goats and wandering sheep not vehicles. We inch our way along arriving at a delightful wide sandy beach and see surfers riding the walloping waves in a town called Inch.

Barbara
The Tart with the Cart

That's what Dubliners call the famous statue of Molly Malone with her pushcart of cockles. This twenty-foot statue in the middle of the City of Dublin fascinates me, Barbara Malone alias Molly Malone. It still amazes me that I, one of the few Italian girls in high school, was selected to play the role of Molly Malone in an operetta. I acted and sang with a brogue. Was it prophetic that I would eventually become Mrs. Malone? I pose with the statue of Molly, looking like a modern day peddler although my decollete' is not as revealing as hers, this morning.

Dick
Sheep, Sheep, Sheep

"Get your hairy asses out of the road," curses Dick who is driving our van on the left side of the road. The sheep are everywhere, on the mountains, in the valleys and in the road blocking our van. We stop and watch the plodding procession of curly-haired sheep. Finally, a sheep dog appears and chases the sheep off the road. Dick entertains us with his endless supply of sheep jokes.

"I'd like to take a picture of the sheep, Dick," I say as we climb a mountain. He stops the car but these sheep are all sleeping. "BAA, BAA," Dick bellows in his rich baritone voice. The sheep lift their heads to look at him.

"I'll take the picture, Barbara. You stand next to the sheep." Dick snaps the picture of two kinky curly heads together, the sheep and me.

"You didn't know you had relatives in Ireland too, did you Barbara?" I'm the only non-Irishman in the group. We all had a good laugh.

Carol & Helen
Hanging From the Cliff in Clifton

"Let's try this farmhouse in Clifton. It's advertised as 'spectacular ocean view'," said Helen, our guide for Bed and Breakfast Inns. We all agree. The sun is shining, Tom is driving and we are jubilant. What can go wrong? Our mood transforms into darkness when Tom drives on a narrow cliffhanger of a lane—Skye Way Road. We are hugging the edge of the lane in our cumbersome van. There is no way to turn back. This continues for a long half-hour. One false move—just inches—and we will tumble over the steep cliff into the rocky ocean.

Carol and Helen are stiff, frozen with fright. I am praying the rosary. I stuff an extra pair of rosary beads into Carol's hands. This is a roller coaster ride with hair-pin turns and heart-stopping action, especially when a car approaches from the opposite direction. When we arrive we shake ourselves out and look at our surroundings. The view is 'spectacular'!

"This farmhouse is G.U., geographically undesirable. It is too far from a pub and definitely not a road to traverse after drinking a Black and Tan ale," agree the men. We gear ourselves up for the Pepcid AC-Tums ride back to the town. When seated in P.J. King's Pub for a pint and relaxation

Carol says, "We are city people." Everyone agreed with her.

Helen & Carol
Tea on the Road to Connemara

We are driving to Connemara through a desert of rocks, no foliage, no buildings, no animals, just a mountain with endless rocks. During the monotony an oasis appears—a coffee shop. We pull in. Tom, Jack and Dick sit at an outdoor table and order tea. Tom pours—they all drink tea. Helen and Carol stop laughing long enough to sip their spring water. Watching Tom drink tea is like watching a grizzly bear drink a cappuccino. This is a first for Tom; his usual beverage is beer.

"Look, there's a sign—Malone's Butcher Shop," says Tom when we arrive in the next town. Tom and I enter the small shop looking for his ancestors. The Malone proprietor tells us, "The Malones come from all over."

Carol & Jack
Seaside Anniversary Dinner

We are in Waterville, a seaside village. It is Carol and Jack's 40th wedding anniversary. We breathe in the refreshing salty air on our walk to the Huntsman Restaurant. The occasion calls for a special celebration. We are in elegant surroundings and are served sumptuous food from attentive waiters.

"I'm in the mood for oysters," says Tom. He requests oysters and he got them. We all ate oysters; Oysters Rockefeller, Oysters Florentine and Garlic Oysters. We savored every bite. We also dine on roast duck, shrimp on curry rice, fresh crab and vegetables.

"To Carol and Jack, may you have many more happy years of

marriage," we toasted with fine wine. We have a panoramic view of the water and the mountains from our linen—silver—china—crystal covered table.

When sated we walk along the one street ocean view village road. The wind is biting as the daylight lingers until ten p.m. I feel like we are in an Agatha Christie novel.

'A semi-deserted European seaside resort off-season populated with characters'. We qualify as the characters—Americans on the Prowl!

Helen
Blarney Castle

"You abandoned us," said Helen in a controlled voice to her husband Dick.

"I've been looking everywhere for you," he replied.

"Helen, how hard could he have looked?" Tom joins in trying to stir up trouble.

"Yes, how hard could you have looked," she repeats raising her voice.

"You always told me that if we ever get separated to wait at the last place we were together."

"Hey, Dick, Barbara and I joined Helen and waited an hour for you to show up. We didn't leave because Helen was sure you'd be back where you left her," chimed in Tom.

This misty morning begins with a long walk up curved narrow steps to the top of Blarney Castle. Tom and I are the only brave ones, of our group, to bend over backwards over a deep forge to kiss the Blarney Stone. In this upside down position I scrape my nose.

"The Irish Blarney Stone is not meant for Roman noses," jokes Tom and we laugh together.

We inhale the freshness of the view of the park from the high castle height. A sea of deep greens and bright whites reveal calla lilies dancing among manicured grass and evergreen trees.

Descending the spiral staircase we meet Helen at the bottom. She has become separated from Dick, Carol and Jack. We waited and waited for the three Irishmen, who we discover later, never went up the stairs to kiss the Blarney Stone. 'Soft rain' descends on us as we are waiting. Mrs. Renaud at the Bed and Breakfast told us that they only have 'soft rain' in Ireland.

"Soft rain doesn't get you wet," she says in her rich Irish brogue, with a twinkle in her eye. When I tired of waiting and was thoroughly drenched by the 'soft rain' I left our post and began searching for our friends. They were warm, comfortable and dry in the van in the parking lot.

Our only mishap on this two-week journey was easily forgiven and forgotten over a Guinness and a Stout in the Black Swan Pub that evening.

Helen
Irish Roots

This morning is shrouded in mist. We hope it burns off.

"There are at least two hours when you can go out and about," says the young Irish lad at the gas station in Glen Beigh. We are looking for Helen's cousin, Phillip McGillicutty. We arrive at Dooks Golf Course. Helen's second cousin, Young Phillip, a red headed freckle-faced Irishman is in the pro shop. He greets us, the American visitors and cousin Helen heartily. We tour this first-class golf course in the 'soft rain'. This rain does not stop the many golfers who are playing among the spectacle of mountains on one side and lush greens sloping down to the ocean on the other. With directions in hand we travel to visit Old Phillip. He lives in a modest white cottage surrounded by a white wall, multi-colored flowers and several horse barns. Old Phillip looks like a leprechaun; short, squat, ruddy-faced, sprightly and friendly. He is overjoyed to see us. His stoic house-dressed wife brought us into their small home and showed us pictures of their eight children and twenty-nine grandchildren. Helen has McGuillicutty cousins all over Ireland.

"We don't have many visitors from across the pond in America," said Old Phillip. We are enjoying their hospitality and opportunity to see the inside of an Irish cottage. When we leave Old Phillip says to Tom, "Don't forget to say hello to Walter, your neighbor in Buttonwoods. Remind him of the girl he left behind in Ireland." He has a glint in his eyes and a chuckle in his voice as he waves us away. Old Phillip is part owner of Dooks Golf Course and owns six thoroughbred race horses. For all his riches he lives humbly.

More Irish roots—Jack's relatives came from Bantry where we didn't see one Daley sign. Murphy signs are everywhere especially in Dublin where the Murphy's Irish Open golf tournament is playing and we cannot get a hotel room. We discover that Helen and Carol both have grandmothers named O'Sullivan from Ireland, who settled in Fox Point, R.I.

Pals, People, Pubs

Everyone agrees that the most enjoyable part of our trip is meeting the Irish folks and relatives, drinking beer and socializing in the pubs and especially the fun we six friends have together.

Every Irishman we meet is gracious, helpful, friendly and remarkably entertaining. For example, we meet Jerry McCarthy at a Bed and breakfast

Inn where we are staying. He captivates us with his historical stories mixed in with a bit of blarney over breakfast.

"Carol is a McCarthy, Jerry," we chorused.

"Welcome home to the tribe," he tells her. He regales us further with some fantastic tales about the McCarthys, St. Patrick and the Lusitania. He is a historian.

"The people built a fort to protect themselves from marauders from the sea. They built it in the wrong place and couldn't see the harbour. Had to build another one."

"We linger and listen to every Irishman we meet; at the B & B's, in the restaurants, on the streets and especially in the pubs. Big decisions are made in the pubs.

"Shall we have a Black and Tan, a Harp, Smithwicks, Guinness, Murphy's, Kilkenney, Beamish, Paddy's and Ginger or Paddy and Soda?"

Lunch in the pubs was fresh, filling and delicious. This is accompanied by live traditional music many days. In the evening the pub is a gathering place for Irishmen of all ages, babies, toddlers, children and adults.

Looking for Honk's

We are told to go to a popular pub called Honk's for great entertainment. We drive and drive and see only wheat fields. Then, it appears, down a dirt lane, just like in the movie 'Field of Dreams', in the middle of nowhere. The pub is pulsating with traditional live music; fiddles, flutes, violins, tin whistles. The young male long-sleeved white shirted musicians are mesmerizing us with their enchanting music. The pub is crowded with people playing darts and cards and pool; talking, drinking and listening to the music. We embraced the throng of noisy revelers and never saw anyone drunk. When I ordered a glass of water from the Irish colleen with the musical lilt in her voice, typical of every Irishman we met, she called out to the bartender, "One Adams Ale." and she brought me water.

Jack and Carol, Dick and Helen, Tom and me—our friendship has deepened and flourished on this trip. God has blessed us with valuable friends, on this journey of life, who support us in stressful times and celebrate in sunny times. We will continue to have many hours of fun together in the future, whether it is on a travel vacation or a dinner of spaghetti and meatballs at the Blessed House. These friends are Just Like Family!

Book V

Fifty Years of Marriage

Amen, I say to you, whatever you did for one
Of these least brothers of mine, you did for Me.

CHAPTER 26
Easter Renewal

There is a time for everything

A time to plant

A time to nourish

A time to grow

A time for change.

High spirits reign at the dinner table on this holy holiday in the Blessed House. For the first time, Cathleen, my oldest daughter revives her gourmet cooking skills in my kitchen. They have been dormant for the past ten years. She places tempting platters of baked spiral ham, steaming macaroni and cheese and a green bean casserole in the middle of the dining room table. Everyone is talking, eating, drinking and enjoying each others company. My grandchildren are poking and joking with each other throughout the meal, just like always. Every Easter the family travels from Massachusetts, Connecticut and Rhode Island to gather for a feast at our house.

"Cathleen, this ham is delicious," exclaims Steven. "We rarely have ham."

"My favorite is this creamy macaroni and cheese. This is the best," says my grandson Sean.

"I didn't even know Aunty Cathy knew how to cook," piped in his sister Emily.

"Cathy was a great cook for many years, before you were born Emily. She was always creating her own recipes," clarified her father, Mike.

"You can cook for me anytime Cathy," says my son Dennis.

This year I did not cook and serve Antipasto and Lasagna.

Steven, our resident caretaker and Tommy our temporary lodger recuperating from a poignant divorce join forces today to tidy up the house for the guests.

This year I did not organize and prepare this Easter dinner.

Paper plates and cups are refilled frequently with succulent food and drink. Paper napkins and plastic tablecloth cover the dining table.

This year I did not place the antique china, crystal and sterling silverware on the linen tablecloth.

"Let's all go visit my new house before we have dessert," suggests my daughter Susan.

"Yeah, Sean we can walk to my house from here now. It's just up the street. No more long ride for me anymore," said my grandson Bobby as the two grandsons lead the exodus. The folks are unanimous that Susan and Bobby's new house is cozy and unique; three staggered levels, hand painted flowers and birds on the floor and walls of the sun porch, three fireplaces, a large master bathroom Jacuzzi and a tree house on the acre of wooded land. They agree it's also very convenient.

Tom and I have not seen their new house.

Back at our house an abundance of desserts appear, as usual. A potpourri of chocolate desserts from Federal Hill Bakery brought by my brother Richard; a cheesecake with bright red cherries made by my sister Beverly and a homemade birthday cake baked by Stephanie, my daughter-in-law are spread across the table. Everyone sings Happy Birthday Dennis before eating the chocolate frosted cake covered with multicolored M & M's and chocolate candy.

This year I did not bake Easter Rice pie, apple and blueberry pie or Dennis' birthday cake.

Over coffee and dessert, plans are made to give a Fiftieth Anniversary Party to Tom and me in the Blessed House. My brother takes portraits of my six children and of my three grandchildren for a surprise anniversary gift to us.

This year Tom and I are not present for this thirtieth Easter celebration in our home. We are vacationing in Florida.

Telephone conversations with our family during dinner confirm the gaiety and bonding of our family.

"Grandma, we miss you."

"When are you coming home?"

"How come you never cook ham, Mom?" Everyone had second helpings."

"Can't talk too long. Got to eat dessert."

"Bye, gotta go, love you Mom and Dad," they chime in together.

The outpouring of love and support for Tommy, at this tumultuous time in his life, is graciously received and helped to restore him.

This year The Blessed House gives it's blessings to my family: bringing peace to a family crises and tightening family bonds even though Tom and I are not present.

There is a time for everything.

There is a time to accept change.

CHAPTER 27
What Not To Do On Your 50th Wedding Anniversary Celebrations

The Gondola…The Cruise…The Party
The Invitation

Happy Anniversary Barbara and Tom
In honor of your 50 happy years together
Jack, Carol, Dick and Helen invite you for a
Venetian Gondola ride on the Providence
Water Place Canal and dinner at the Pot a Fuer
Restaurant on a day of your choice.

DON'T indulge in two glasses of champagne riding in an authentic Venetian Gondola and eat savory Bouillabaisse at the French restaurant if you are going to faint and be carted off in an ambulance while your hosts are still eating dinner.

DON'T lie on a Gurney for two hours waiting for the doctor to see you while your friends linger in the emergency waiting room because you all traveled together in one car.

DO promise never to drink champagne or alcohol on an empty stomach again when all medical tests are normal.

DO accept your friends mocking:

"Barbara, we know you enjoy being the Drama Queen."

"Isn't this overkill?"

"I think you're just looking for material for your book."

DO thank your friends for their generosity, friendship and patience as you delight in the cruise down the canal seated in a velvet cushioned black and gold gondola while the Gondolier paddles along serenading you with Italian love songs.

DO hang their magnificent gift of a large canvas painting of a white sailboat with shades of gold on the blue-green Aegean Sea with white stucco Greek-style houses in the foreground, on your newly painted white kitchen wall.

DO go rummaging through the garbage of coffee grounds and banana peels to find the sales receipt so you can iron, fold and return the recently purchased and hung Tuscan-style curtains and decorations that clash with the painting.

The Cruise Brochure
Turkey Explorer

* 2 nights Istanbul, 5 nights Greek Island Cruise, 2 nights Athens.

DON'T book a Mediterranean Cruise on a low-budget bottom level cabin in the ship's bow with separated bunk beds next to the anchor if you expect romance on the high seas with your Golden Anniversary lover.

DON'T scream, *"The ship is crashing, we're breaking up,"* as you jump on top of your husband in his narrow bed when the loud clanging of the heavy chain lowering the anchor jolts you awake in the middle of the night.

DON'T blame the ship's Captain for the turbulent waters that slam into the ship keeping you awake and preventing you from docking on the island of Mykonos.

DON'T leave your charger at home if you intend to take many once-in-a-lifetime pictures with your new Anniversary present digital camera.

DON'T buy a sealed Kodachrome disposable camera for too many Euros at a tourist trap in Turkey when your battery wears down…camera taped together.

DON'T forget your umbrella if you don't want to be dripping wet when you make a pilgrimage to the sacred house of the Blessed Virgin Mary on the mountaintop in Ephesus, Turkey.

DON'T take out travel insurance hoping you don't have an accident like our fully insured friend Jack who had the misfortune of tripping while exiting a rocking ship to the tender boat and being transferred to a hospital, then flown home or you'll have to suffer and pay big Euro bucks.

DO give support to Carol because she has to listen to Jack's grumblings as he lies immobilized in the antiquated mash-style-open-ward barracks at a Greek hospital overnight with no TV, no radio, no towels, no soap and basin, no call bell or urinal…bathroom down the hall.

DON'T wear shorts when you visit the Blue Mosque in Turkey or you will have to have the attendant wrap you in a long skirt, like Jack and Dick.

DON'T sail the Greek Islands in late October, lower rates, if you expect to go swimming in the Topside pool—no water, or sunning in a deck lounge chair—too cool and windy.

DO wear comfortable shoes as you walk through the archeological wonders of the Byzantine and Ottoman Empires in the Hippodrome,

Blue Mosque, St. Sophia Museum and the Topaki Palace in Istanbul.

DO bargain with the Turkish sellers of wares in the Grand Bazaar, a maze of 4000 shops filled with antiques, jewelry, carpets, leather, etc.— the largest mall in the world.

DO enjoy the lavish 5 star hotels in Istanbul and Athens.

DO relish the gourmet meals 5 times a day with unique Greek and Turkish spices as well as the Ruby Band and Entertainers every evening in the Sirenes Lounge on the ship.

DO breathe in the salty smells and watch the ever present sunshine bounce on the water from the open deck of the ship, Ruby, with your best friends who are traveling with you on your Anniversary journey.

DO trust the Greek man in the hi-tech camera shop in the ancient walled city of Rhodes to charge your camera battery while you explore several thousand years of history on this "Island of Roses."

DO explore the extraordinary island of Santorini from below or at the Tike Bar when you renege on going up the steep ancient volcano in a glass enclosed Tramway or on a donkey.

DO not give up after walking for hours in Athens looking for the Plaka so you can recapture memories of dancing and drinking all night, 35 years ago!

DO have a good time with your friends and laugh often.

The Party Invitation

A postcard of sea-blue green waters and the words…
You are invited to a 50th
Wedding Anniversary Celebration
for Tom and Barbara Malone
at their home on August 31, 2007
NO GIFTS

DON'T interfere with your six children, spouses and grandchildren's well choreographed plans to honor you at a memorable Golden Wedding Anniversary party for family and fifty of your friends at your Blessed House.

DON'T question your daughter's choices of no RSVP on the invitation… *"Mom, you know everyone always comes to your parties in this house."*…because they will come.

DON'T keep insisting that you will do all the cooking because you enjoy cooking for family and friends.

DO accept that a renowned caterer has been engaged but you can make your signature dish of Lasagna if it makes you happy.

DO compliment your sons and daughters on their creative spirit and energy that transforms the Blessed House, deck and yard into a magical golden palace with a myriad of shimmering golden decorations, wedding bells, dozens of white and red roses and 50 gold and white balloons blowing in the wind.

DO accept that your family has no control over the weather for this indoor-outdoor event and that the warm sunshine with high winds off the water will tug at the gold tablecloths and melt the heart shaped ice-sculptures with red roses inside, much too soon.

DO enjoy the celebration of 50 years of marriage and 30 years in the Blessed House mingling with family and friends while bartenders and waitresses serve you and the guests without your help.

DO pose for pictures with your husband, family and friends that your sister, son and daughter are taking even though the salty wind wraps your skirt around your legs and twists your hair into a birds nest.

DO let your husband take the lead after you cut and eat a piece of the 3 tired wedding cake when guests ask how we met, since you are not prepared to speak.

DON'T be intimidated by the silent guests…your husband looks over at your 50 year old winkled wedding gown hanging by the window and begins… *"Barbara has held up much better these years than her wedding gown."*

DO accept that as a compliment even though you still have trouble appreciating his Irish humor after all these years.

Tom… *"When I met Barbara at a Rhode Island Hospital Nurses Dance she didn't have her eyeglasses on."*

Heckler #1… *"She still doesn't have her eyeglasses on, no wonder she's still with you."*

Heckler #2… *"Barbara, I thought you were engaged to someone else when you met Tom. Why did you pick Tom?"*

Barbara… *"Because he was a better kisser!"* a spontaneous answer that should have been given more thought.

Tom… *"How I met Barbara…hmmm*

I was a student at Providence College and I told my friend Jack, the Ladies man, that a notice on the bulletin board announced a dance at the Nurses Home on Saturday night. I worked at the Fence Co. that Saturday and I was exhausted. I went to bed forgetting about the dance. My friend Jack called my house repeatedly and my mother finally told me to answer the phone and give Jack an answer. I tried to get out of it but Jack persisted and I reluctantly went to the dance. Jack, the ladies man, danced with all the girls. When I saw Barbara sitting alone I got up the courage to ask her to dance. At the end of the evening she told me she was engaged to a guy in Korea and he gave her permission to date as long as she didn't get serious about anyone. I thought—great— I don't want commitment. I have too many more years of college and law school ahead of me."

Heckler #3… *"How patriotic of you, Tom—dating Soldierboy's girl while he's off fighting for our country."*

Barbara… *"How I met Tom…*

I was a second year student in nursing school and Social Director of the Dances that year. I invited my friend Joan, the Bridesmaid, to come to our hospital dance and visit overnight. Beautiful, tall, Joan danced all night although there was a scarcity of men that night. I was sitting at a table with five nurses. One by one each girl was asked to dance. I had been sitting down all night. When there were two of us left I said to her, "If I don't get asked to dance soon, I am going up to bed." She danced. I sat alone. Finally Tom asked me to dance. I was thrilled and we danced all night. When I went up to bed with Joan I asked her… "What does he look like?" I did not have my eyeglasses on. She answered, "He looks pleasant enough."

"After one or two dates I knew Tom was the man I wanted to marry. He lit a fire in my heart and it's been burning ever since. I didn't want to scare him away. In the meantime I wrote subtle notes to Soldierboy in Korea trying to break the news gently."

Heckler #4… *"Barbara, you wrote a Dear John letter! Shame on you!"*

Heckler #5… *"Poor Soldierboy is risking his life for us."*

Barbara… *"O.K. I did write a Dear John letter, sort of. I wrote that I had something important to tell him when he came home. Then I quit writing love letters. The night Soldierboy unexpectedly arrived at the nurses residence I was on a date with a sailor."*

Heckler #6… *"You dated a soldier and a sailor and you settled for a draft-dodger?"*

Barbara… *"Tom was in college. Anyway, my three best friends met me at the bus stop and walked with us to the nurses residence whispering in my ear…*

"Your Soldierboy is waiting for you in the Nurses home. Get rid of the sailor."

Entangling myself from an awkward situation I walked into a hot-bed. I told Soldierboy that I loved someone else and could not marry him. I was torn apart when he was on his knees in the dating parlor, crying and begging me to change my mind. He was a very nice guy. I did not get away with it easily. I felt guilty and my nurse friends who loved Soliderboy were very angry with me. I did not get welcomed with open arms by Tom. He insisted he wasn't interested in marriage. He wanted to finish his education. He told me to forget him and marry Soldierboy.

Three years, two poems and many love letters later, we married at the Presentation of the Blessed Virgin Mary Church with my sister Beverly, the Maid of Honor, Tom's brother Edward, the Best Man, and my friend Joan, the Bridesmaid, and Jack, the Ladies Man, as Tom's usher. 50 years later, we owe Joan the Bridesmaid and Jack the Ladies Man our thanks.

DON'T forget to send your husband a 50th Anniversary card, if you expect him to renew his wedding vows with you and the Bishop in the Cathedral of St. John and Paul.

DON'T eat one-half of the left-over 3 tier wedding cake the next day if you don't want to be sick.

My Tom

He has the reddest nose around
The biggest bluest eyes I've found
A boy so gentle and so kind
And yet he never is on time.
That's my Tom!

He played the best football in school
In every sport he knows the rule
A sports enthusiast is he
But can he drive? Oh, woe is me!

He studies hard, strives for his goal
No handyman is he at home
He'll stay awake as late as three
But sleeps 'til noon so easily
That's my Tom!

A reassuring word from him
Makes my life no longer dim
He can thrill me with a glance
White T-shirt and khaki pants
That's my Tom!

Romantic lover he can be
Or lose his temper over me
His voice sends out the sweetest songs
And I could never get along
Without my Tom!

Barbara Olean
'1955'

The Poems

"Forget Me."

You left me standing there alone
With these two words, "Forget Me."
As if I ever could.

As if your face so clean and fine
As if the smell of shaving lotion
As if your kisses that were mine
Could ever be forgotten.

As if your phone calls giving me cheer
As if the times you've called me darling
As if your arms that held me near
Could ever be forgotten.

As if my love was a passing fancy
You cast me aside and said "Forget Me."
As if I ever could.

Barbara Olean
'1955 '

My Tom

Red nose, blue eyes, plus bright green hat
He looks the same, just add more fat
Gentle, kind and patient too
If you don't tell him what to do!
That's my Tom!

Season tickets, Winter and Fall
Football, hockey and basketball
Golf he plays in Spring and Summer
I can't think of anything dumber!
That's my Tom!

With six children we have been blessed
He's King at home, by now you've guessed
Studies, Jobs, he's had so many
Sometimes we have naught a penny
That's my Tom!

His charm and wit make him unique
When I'm with him I'm at my peak
As Lover, Father, Everyone's Friend
He succeeds so very well
That's my Tom!

After 15 years I will keep my Tom!
Barbara Malone
'1972'

Amen, I say to you, whatever you did for one of
these least brothers of mine, you did for me.

CHAPTER 28
Past and Present

I rush out to the back porch in my red and white polka dot bandana. I am wearing my navy and white striped tee shirt and white shorts to greet my husband returning from his golf game. As I lean over the railing smiling my husband said,

"You look pretty as a picture smiling next to the flag with your red bandana and the flag waving in the wind." He raced into the house while shouting,

"Don't move," and got the camera. I was surprised because his picture-taking and compliments are not common occurrences.

Fifty years ago I was smiling too, in all the pictures on Tom's and my wedding day. We were both excited as we anticipated living together as husband and wife.

From thirty years ago I am picturing Tom's and my smiling faces as we stand on the front lawn of our new house overlooking the sweeping expanse of Greenwich Bay waters. We're excited about living here with our family. We didn't know then that this former Priest's house was a

Blessed House. We only knew that we lived in a special place. Along our journey of life's twists and turns we were guided by the Lord's hand. When my husband lost his job, we had two children in college and a new mortgage, yet he was able to find and finance a new business. When we needed help to renovate the house after firing three incompetent carpenters, a skilled craftsman was recommended to us. Working as a psychotherapist I received inspiration from the Lord as to what to say to clients who came to my home-office in distress. Two of our sons, at times, suffered physically or emotionally and were led to healing and peace. Divine grace was given to family members whose relationships were tenuous or dissolved by divorce, death or desertion so we could reach renewal and acceptance. When Tom and I prayed together for more inner-strength and patience the Lord answered our prayers.

A few things are different now.

The beach has washed away
The children have left home
The clams are petering out
The clients come no more.
Still
The holy walls are standing
The love and blessings abound
On those who live and visit
The Blessed House by the shore.

The panorama has changed for our family and our home. Cathleen, a special education Teacher of the Year who lives and teaches in Connecticut, visits with friends and bring their dogs. Michael, a C.P.A.

drives from Massachusetts with his wife Stephanie, an R.N., thirteen year old Boy Scout-baseball player son, Sean and eleven year old daughter Emily, an equestrian and budding writer. Steven, who works at the family business, is our resident caretaker when we vacation and can solve any technical and mechanical problems for family and friends. Susan, a successful business woman lives in the neighborhood with her son Bobby who just learned to drive a car and has been dirt-bike racing for years. Tommy, a truck driver for a non-profit food bank, lives close by and recently became engaged to Katie who has two children, Tony and Jonathan. Dennis, our youngest, excels as the acting C.E.O. of the family business and lives nearby in his own home. I am grateful that my family has absorbed and practices Tom and my values: love, family, spirituality, work, fun and kindness to others.

For all the changes many things are the same at the Blessed House. Tom and I both live, love, cook and entertain family and friends. The Blessed House is still a gathering place. Holidays are still celebrated here. Christmas is still a momentous event with the family meeting to exchange presents around a huge Christmas Tree in the living room that we cut down every year. Camp Grandma brings our vacationing grandchildren to eat, swim and play games with us. The 4th of July Malone—Murphy—Daley Party is still a jubilation adding new spouses as their children marry and more grandchildren are born. The Buttonwoods Resort is still hosting our Ohio relatives and sometimes my nurse friends. I still go quahogging in front of the house. It takes a lot longer to rake enough clams for the linguini and stuffies I cook for family and friends.

The welcoming couches on the porch are filled with people talking; music floats in over the ceiling speakers, and grandchildren and adults are playing Hi-Lo-Jack or Scrabble. The lounge chairs on the deck are full, some people reading, others sunbathing. Sometimes Tom is grilling burgers on the living room grille or I am cooking spaghetti and meatballs in the kitchen. In the same room where the Priest changed bread and wine into the body and blood of Christ, we break bread daily on our dining room table. We add extensions to the table on holidays as the family expands every year. The large swamp maple and mulberry trees cast a cooling shade on the house and front lawn. The house has a settled look and the outer walls that were constructed from a demolished church are still the backbone of the house.

The erosion is halted. The rock wall is holding fast. Reinforcements have been made. The house is safe. Hope is alive. I continue to swim and quahog but now I must climb over the rocks or walk through my next door neighbors yard. Clambakes are now cooked on a grate at the edge of the lawn. Our bedroom-sitting room continues to be well-used. Summer sea breezes flow through the floor-to-ceiling windows, so we sleep well. Although sometimes I am distracted by the boats and marine life in my windows, I enjoy writing at my desk and meditating and praying in the love seat facing the view of God's creations. Peace settles into my soul.

Thirty years ago the house was filled with teenage noise: telephones ringing, rock music blaring and yelling back and forth.

"What time is baseball practice tomorrow?"

"Be quiet, I'm trying to do my homework."

"Shut your door."

"What do you think about that new girl in school?"

I remember the time Tommy sailed the sunfish. It was overloaded with teenage girls. When he got lost in the fog the irate parents lined up on the shore in front of our house. Other memories flood over me. The house hosted many celebrations through the years: birthdays, graduations, baby and wedding showers, Confirmation and a Mass. Those noisy days passed when Tom drove to his steady job in Providence, the children were bused to a neighborhood school and I cloistered myself in my home-office with clients. The house was becoming quieter.

Today, the house seems almost silent. I retired from counseling after twenty-five years and Tom works part-time at his manufacturing business and the children are grown. Yet, the house embraces us with comfort as we read, talk, write and listen to music; for in this Blessed House with its now silent rooms I still hear the laughter and see the faces of family and friends. The silence is broken on holidays, special occasions and summertime when we entertain. The house resounds with the talk and laughter of children, spouses, grandchildren, relatives and friends. The five bedrooms are filled with family from out-of-town: Ohio, Massachusetts and Connecticut.

The house spoke to me thirty years ago.

"Change this house into a family home."

We succeeded in transforming the Priest's house into a home for our family beginning with ripping the inside walls down to insert new electrical, plumbing and insulation, then putting the original pine paneling back together again. These walls still hold the spirits of the Lord's blessings. This seaside community Rev. Bixby founded for summer relaxation and religious retreat is still an exceptional place to live. The Buttonwoods Beach Chapel, the 130 year old cornerstone of the community continues to host weddings, anniversaries and non-denominational religious services. The historic Casino is still a hub of activity: tennis, bowling, dances and parties for residents of all ages. Rev. Bixby left his intrinsic values of religion and neighbors helping neighbors, young and old in our neighborhood.

The house speaks to me.

"Be generous. Give away your precious gift of time, energy and love to all who come to me, family, friends, guests."

This is my call to life. This is what I have been doing for thirty years. This house was built for Nourishment, Conversation, Laughter, Prayer and Reflection. The Lord has blessed us with good health, good family, good friends and a comfortable home. We rejoice and thank Him.

I look around me. Surrounded by my family and friends I pause for a moment. Gazing at the view through our windows I am still overwhelmed by the magnitude of God's harmonious creation: from the multicolored butterfly feasting on the periwinkle blue flowering weeds at the lawn's edge, to the schools of silver baby skip jack blue fish that glide and sometimes jump out of the water altogether. How privileged I am to live here feeling His presence so close. I marvel at an Almighty God who gives us such beauty and miracles to enjoy every day. I feel His warmth as the sun's rays awaken me in our curtainless bedroom. Through the day the waves sing as they crash onto the rock wall and then retreat with the tide. Above the seagulls fly and cry into the wind. A lush sunset, first oranges, then reds, sometimes purples and blues reflects in the water as the day draws to a close. My awe persists, my love deepens, my faith and hope keep renewing. I am still at peace. Tom and my long-lasting love continues to grow. We are happy in this Blessed House.

The house speaks.

"I'm always at my best when family and friends congregate to break bread together."

Has the house been speaking to me all these years? Or is it the spirit of those who have gone before me in this seaside community? Or is it Father St. Jean, who built this house and lived and died in it so many years ago who is guiding me to carry on his work?

EPILOGUE
One Year and Four Months Later

E-MAIL

from—MOM

address—BLESSED HOUSE

To—STEVEN

address—HEAVEN

subject—A LOVE LETTER TO MY SON

This Easter Sunday, the feast of Christ's resurrection into Heaven, our family is gathered around the table in the Blessed House to remember you, Steven, and to celebrate your moving on to another life, a peaceful life with no more pain, a life with Jesus in Heaven.

This is the spot where we gather for family meals, weddings, reunions, Confirmations, graduations and, more recently, your tear-stained funeral luncheon. We know it was you, Steve, that flicked the chandelier on and off during that luncheon. We realize you were telling us that you were O.K. Thanks.

We are surrounded by three large posters of photos of you, with poignant captions that your sister's Cathy and Susan designed for the grief-stricken—that they would know about your precious life. Your sisters decided that the Steven Posters would accompany us at all our future celebrations in the Blessed House. You are missed Steven, but live on in my heart as I remember the immense joy you brought to me, your family and friends throughout your all too-brief life.

You made my life easier because you were a quiet, happy child in the middle of your spirited brothers and sisters. With an unwavering smile on your face, you busied yourself with toys (driving your red fire engine) and later with mechanical objects and cars. You took apart our new rotor-roof antenna at a young age. We were baffled. You said, "How was I going to know how it worked?"

As you matured you welcomed even more challenges and conquered most everything you attempted. I was in awe as I watched you undertake your first project; building a car from two junk-yard wrecks before you had your driver's license and then driving it down the street.

Your self-taught technical and mechanical skills were paramount. You began by repairing cars and later moving on to computers. You were so generous with your time and talents. Everyone benefitted—family and friends. Besides repairing our cars, you took the time to take everyone car-shopping when the need arose. You built computers, repaired them, gave us advice on buying one and taught us how to use them.

"What needs fixing now?" you'd ask, because this old house and appliances always needed repairs. You saved us so much money. I was shocked when you fixed our thirty year old compactor after the repair man said to throw it out.

When Dad bought the hammer business, you surprised us all by creating and designing an efficient system for making lead hammers. Throughout the years, you made all the repairs on all the large machinery in the family business. You took on more challenges, developing carpentry, plumbing and electrical skills when Dad bought a worn-down Laundromat. Dad could not have done these businesses without your help. We are both so grateful.

I was so touched when you took the time to reach out to some mentally challenged people who needed help on the job and with their life. You even socialized with them as well as bringing them home for Thanksgiving. I am proud of you son, because you are sensitive and caring to those less fortunate.

"Be passionate," you frequently told Dad and me. You were so passionate about everything, whether in discussions about politics, sports, science, your deep religious faith or when you were teaching someone how to do calculus, repair a car or the technical advances in computers. I marveled at the breadth of your knowledge.

Your greatest passion was for your family. You were kind and generous and readily available when you were well. When Dennis needed help converting the old Addressograph billing system into the computer, you were there. When your nephew Bobby wanted an expert mechanic to help him lift his truck in order to add oversize tires, you were there.

"I really had fun working with Bobby and his father," you confided.

When Dennis needed a new kitchen sink and bathroom fixtures, you were there. It was important for you to be a 'good brother' and a 'good son' and, believe me, you were the best, Steven. You brought joy to so many.

Tommy said he'd never forget the things you did together and what you taught him. You built his first computer, taught him how to operate it and eventually to build his own computer. You forced him to do his own research and figure things out for himself. He is grateful and gives you credit for his new career in computers, and also for teaching him how to do his own maintenance on his cars.

Tommy and Dad were amazed at your ability to come up with things that are unconventional. You really thought outside-the-box and it paid off. Like the time you took Tommy's truck and incompatible junk yard parts of trucks to build him a working dump truck for his landscaping business. Everything was a challenge to you. We all appreciated your genius.

You were a wonderful companion to Dad, taking walks, having discussions, and doing projects around the house, garage and shop together. Dad enjoyed watching you do your 'magic tricks,' as he called them. He knew you had a gift to see the whole by looking at the pieces. Some days, when you were suffering with Crohn's disease you could not get out of bed. I wished I could take away your pain. You researched your disease and took an active role in your treatment. You endured many set-backs, bowel surgery and several medication changes that did not work, yet you never gave up hope. You had great plans for the future. You and Dennis discussed ways to improve the family business and you had your bags packed for a winter vacation with us in Florida.

Last fall you had a brief respite from your pain and delighted Tom and me with your playful personality and high energy when you visited our Florida vacation home. After you gave our car a thorough mechanical tune-up, you drove Dad and me down to Florida.

"I feel like Happy Gilmore. I'm having so much fun. It's like being a kid again," you told us. You gave Dad and me so much pleasure to see you magically transformed; riding a bicycle, swimming and sunning at the beach, picking the fruit on our grapefruit and orange trees, dining at Mel's Diner and Doc's, playing golf with Dad, walking briskly for an hour with me everyday, and appreciating the beauty of this Floridian paradise.

"Save my bed for me. I'm coming back. I can't believe I've been missing this all these years. I'll have to stay a month this winter," you said. I wish you could be with us this winter, Steve, and every winter. I'll miss the real Steve where you were shining as brilliantly as the southern sun. I'm so glad you encouraged me to take pictures of us together when you were here, for our Florida album and yours. In every picture you have a smiling face. What wonderful memories.

Steve, the first time I put on the headphones of your Walkman in order to be close to you, the song playing on your radio was, "We are apart now but our love is still strong." and the chorus kept repeating, "Everything's going to be alright." You sent this *message because you knew I needed to hear it then. Thanks. I know everything is going to be alright now. Our love does not end; it continues and endures. I'll miss you but I will see you again.*

Love, Mom

Father St. Jean lived in the Blessed House and died here after a heart attack. He gave many hours of joy to his parishioners.

Steven lived most of his adult life in the Blessed House and died here of complications of Crohn's disease. He gave many hours of joy to his family and friends.